CAMBRIDGE LIBRARY COLLECTION

Books of enduring scholarly value

Literary studies

This series provides a high-quality selection of early printings of literary works, textual editions, anthologies and literary criticism which are of lasting scholarly interest. Ranging from Old English to Shakespeare to early twentieth-century work from around the world, these books offer a valuable resource for scholars in reception history, textual editing, and literary studies.

Jacke Jugeler

This 1914 scholarly edition of the mid-sixteenth-century play Jacke Jugeler contains an informative introduction and detailed notes. Little-known today, the play represents a pre-Shakespearean example of classical 'borrowing' – a Roman play by Plautus is adapted to an English domestic situation – and it is one of the first instances of confused identity and 'doubles' in English comedy. The text of this edition is taken from the unique original, probably published around 1562, in the collection of the Duke of Devonshire. In his Introduction, W. H. Williams proposes the likely identity of the play's author, and provides an analysis of the play's language to support his claim. He examines the connections in method, characters and language between Jacke Jugeler and Ralph Roister Doister, a play written and performed around the same time.

Cambridge University Press has long been a pioneer in the reissuing of out-of-print titles from its own backlist, producing digital reprints of books that are still sought after by scholars and students but could not be reprinted economically using traditional technology. The Cambridge Library Collection extends this activity to a wider range of books which are still of importance to researchers and professionals, either for the source material they contain, or as landmarks in the history of their academic discipline.

Drawing from the world-renowned collections in the Cambridge University Library, and guided by the advice of experts in each subject area, Cambridge University Press is using state-of-the-art scanning machines in its own Printing House to capture the content of each book selected for inclusion. The files are processed to give a consistently clear, crisp image, and the books finished to the high quality standard for which the Press is recognised around the world. The latest print-on-demand technology ensures that the books will remain available indefinitely, and that orders for single or multiple copies can quickly be supplied.

The Cambridge Library Collection will bring back to life books of enduring scholarly value across a wide range of disciplines in the humanities and social sciences and in science and technology.

Jacke Jugeler

WILLIAM HENRY WILLIAMS

CAMBRIDGE
UNIVERSITY PRESS

CAMBRIDGE UNIVERSITY PRESS

Cambridge New York Melbourne Madrid Cape Town Singapore São Paolo Delhi

Published in the United States of America by Cambridge University Press, New York

www.cambridge.org
Information on this title: www.cambridge.org/9781108002608

© in this compilation Cambridge University Press 2009

This edition first published 1914
This digitally printed version 2009

ISBN 978-1-108-00260-8

JACKE JUGELER

CAMBRIDGE UNIVERSITY PRESS

C. F. CLAY, Manager

London: FETTER LANE, E.C.

Edinburgh: 100 PRINCES STREET

New York: G. P. PUTNAM'S SONS

Bombay and Calcutta: MACMILLAN AND CO., Ltd.

Toronto: J. M. DENT AND SONS, Ltd.

Tokyo: THE MARUZEN-KABUSHIKI-KAISHA

JACKE JUGELER

Edited with Introduction and Notes by

W. H. WILLIAMS, M.A.

Formerly Scholar of Trinity College, Cambridge
Professor of Classics and English Literature in the
University of Tasmania

Cambridge :
at the University Press
1914

Cambridge:

PRINTED BY JOHN CLAY, M.A.
AT THE UNIVERSITY PRESS

CONTENTS

INTRODUCTION[1].

§ 1. TEXT. The text of the present edition is taken from the unique original in the collection of His Grace the Duke of Devonshire, K.G.

§ 2. DATE. In vol. I. p. 202 of Arber's *Transcript of the Registers of the Company of Stationers of London*, 1554–1640 A.D., (corresponding to fol. 85 b of Register A), occurs the following entry:

> Recevyd of William Coplande for his lycense for pryntinge of an interlude intituled Jack Juggeler and mistress Boundgrace   .   . iiij^d

The part of the Register in which this occurs extends from fol. 84 a–92 a, and is headed 'ffor Takynge of ffynes for Copyes as folowethe.' This again is part of the 'accompte made by... Wardens of the Companye of Stacioners of all such sommes of monye as hathe comme to theare handes from the xxijth Daye of July Anno 1562 vnto the xxij of July Anno 1563 which ys by the space of one hole yere as folowethe.'

The 'accompte' for the 12 months fills fol. 82 a–fol. 96 b.

The entry of the payment for *Jack Juggeler* is 36th out of 124. Five entries back is one 'Recevyd of garrard Dewes for his lycense for pryntinge of a pycture of [a] monsterus pygge at Hamsted iiij^d.' Arber's note on this is, 'the broadside is entitled *The description of a monstrous pig, the which was farrowed at Hamsted besyde London, the xvi day of October, the present yeare of our Lord God, MDLxij.*'

---

[1] Part of this Introduction was published in *The Modern Language Review*, July 1912.

W. J. J.   *b*

This, and the comparatively early occurrence of the entry about *Jack Juggeler* (the lists are not alphabetical), suggest that the entry was still in 1562. No. 53 was a payment in respect of *Crestenmas Carroles*. This again points to 1562. It may be added that William Copland issued books with his imprint from 1548 to 1561 (*D.N.B.*).

We may therefore conclude that an edition of *Jack Juggeler* was probably published in the year 1562. The two loose leaves, which by the courtesy of His Grace the Duke of Devonshire are here reproduced, may have belonged to this edition, as the spelling is much later than that of the complete copy, which we shall see reason to believe was written before 1552.

The probability of this assumption depends upon the relation of *Jacke Jugeler* (as we will spell it when referring to the older edition), and *Ralph Roister Doister*.

We may assume that *Ralph Roister Doister* was written in 1552. It is not necessary to discuss the question here, but the reasons may be found in the preface to the edition of the play in the Temple Dramatists (ed. Williams-Robin), pp. v–vii.

What reasons are there for believing that *Jacke Jugeler* was written before *Ralph Roister Doister*?

Whether written by the same person or not, there is evidently a close connexion between the two plays in method, characters, and language.

(*a*) *Method.* Both adapt episodes from Latin comedy to the environment of Tudor London, and embody more or less literal transcripts from Plautus. The prologue of *Ralph Roister Doister* is either a condensed paraphrase of the prologue of *Jacke Jugeler*, or that is an expansion of the main points of the other.

(*b*) *Characters.* Mayster Boungrace corresponds to Gawyn Goodlucke, Dame Coye to Christian Custance, Jacke Jugeler to Mathewe Merygreeke, Jenkyn Careawaye to Truepenie, Ales trype and go to Tibet Talk apace.

(c) *Language.* Among the more obvious resemblances of language may be noted:

Jacke Jugeler	*Ralph Roister Doister*	
69. you shal here a thing y^t onlie shal make you merie & glad.	I. i. 59.	I can when I will make him mery and glad.
137. my cosune Careawaie.	III. i. 4.	my cousin Roister Doister.
148. by cokes prceious (*sic*) potstike.	III. iv. 127.	by cocks precious potsticke.
228. she swimmeth to and fro.	II. iii. 46.	ye shall see hir glide and swimme.
317. saint Gorge ye boroue.	IV. viii. 45.	sainct George to borow.
318. ieopard a ioynt.	IV. viii. 17.	ieoparde my hande.
348. who lustith to feale shall find his hart creping out at his heele.	III. iii. 96.	I might feele your soule departing within an inche of your heele.
430. *In nomine patris.*	I. iv. 49.	*Nomine patris.*
486. Truce for a whyle.	IV. viii. 33.	truce for a pissing while or twaine.
496. beate on mee, tyll I stinke.	IV. iii. 120.	I shall cloute thee tyll thou stinke.
593. by gods precious.	IV. viii. 40	by cocks precious.
615. well curryed.	I. iii. 77.	a curried cote.
640. let me alone.	I. ii. 175.	lette me alone.
726. this wagepastie.	III. ii. 10.	a little wagpastie.
731. the matter lyeth gretylie me a pon.	I. iv. 9.	this lieth vpon his preferment.
861. I shall rape thee.	III. v. 93.	rappe you againe.
976. hence to Jherusalem.	IV. vii. 60.	hennes to grece.
1013. cal ye other his good maister.	IV. vii. 100.	be good maister to her.

If these resemblances are allowed to establish a *prima facie* probability of connexion between the two plays, whether written by the same person or not, which of the two was more likely to be written before the other?

Jacke Jugeler is a one-act farce on the lines of Heywood's interludes, with three scenes (vv. 84–601, 602–773, 774–992), and five characters, needing only three or four performers (if the

b 2

prologue and the epilogue were recited by one), the parts being distributed thus :—1. Careawaye, 2. Jugeler and Dame Coye, 3. Ales and Mayster Boungrace ; or, 1. Careawaye, 2. Jugeler and Ales, 3. Dame Coye, 4. Mayster Boungrace. The time of the action is only an hour, and the place is unchanged.

Ralph Roister Doister is a regularly constructed comedy of five acts subdivided into numerous scenes, with 13 characters requiring as many as 10 actors even if some of the minor parts are combined. The time required for the action is two days. The place, as in *Jacke Jugeler*, need not be changed, the scene being laid before Custance's house, but the characters are more elaborated and individualised than their somewhat sketchy and conventional counterparts.

Which of these then is likely to have preceded the other in order of time, the outline or the finished work ? If they were both written by the same person, probability almost amounts to absolute certainty. In that case *Ralph Roister Doister* can no more have preceded *Jacke Jugeler* than the full corn in the ear can precede the blade, or the fruit the blossom. Was then *Jacke Jugeler* written by the author of *Ralph Roister Doister* ?

§ 3. AUTHOR. The verbal resemblances between *Jacke Jugeler* and *Ralph Roister Doister* would not by themselves prove that the two pieces were composed by the same hand. The author of the one play may have copied from the other. But if we find striking similarities of language between *Jacke Jugeler* and the non-dramatic works of the author of *Ralph Roister Doister* the identity of authorship becomes vastly more probable. Such are :

Jacke Jugeler	*Udall's prose works*
42. And Cicero Tullius............ ....in that his fyrst boke which he wrot, and entytulid, of an honest mans office.	*Apophthegmes*, f. 279, '*Marcus Tullius* in yᵉ thirde booke of that his werke entitleed, *de officiis*, (that is to saie, of honeste behauour, or, how eche manne ought to vse and to demeane hymselfe).'

Jacke Jugeler	*Udall's prose works*
85. Rest you merye.	*Floures*, 'Amice salue. Good felow god you saue, or, o louynge frend god rest you mery.'
108. god before.	*Apoph.* f. 152, 'For the grekes saien σὺν θεοῖς, with the Goddes, for that we saye in englyshe, Goddes pleasure beeyng so, or, by the wyll and grace of God, or, and God before, or, God saiyng amen.'
145. oon faire touche.	*Apoph.* f. 105, 'yea and for a faire touche.'
249. I may giue my life for halpenis three.	*Floures*, 'ego perierim, I am vtterlye vndone, or 1 may gyue my lyfe for an halfepeny.'
293. arayed.	*Erasm. Par. Luke* xiii. 11, 'Araied with a disease.' *Apophth.* f. 315, 'eiuill araied.'
482. no poynt.	*Apoph.* f. 137, 'estemed the fruite to bee no poyncte the more polluted.'
615. curryed.	*Floures*, 'Verberibus casum te, &c. I woll all to currie the, &c.'
657. as sholde be to him a corrasiue.	*Apoph.* f. 154, 'geuen no bodye a corrosif.'
674. breched in suche a brake.	*Erasm. Par. Luke*, Pref. 6 b. 'So should I in this matier stand in a streight brake.'
731. the matter lyeth gretylie me apon.	*Floures*, 'Scin ad te attinere hanc omnem rem? Doest thou remember that all this matter perteyneth to the? or lyeth the vppon?'
908. fauoure your fyste.	*Floures*, 'tibi parce, fauour or spare your selfe.'

If in addition to these resemblances of language we find in *Jacke Jugeler* obviously autobiographical allusions which may be explained by known facts in the life of Udall the probability of his authorship is still further increased.

The facts are as follow. Certain silver images and other plate were alleged to have been stolen from Eton when Udall was

head-master. The matter came before the Privy Council at
Westminster on the 12th of March, 1541/2, when William
Emlar, a goldsmith of London, was examined on the charge of
buying them, 'and beying suspected to have used hym self lewdly
in the handlyng of the matter was committed to the porter's
warde' (Nicolas, *Proceedings and Ordinances of the Privy Council*,
vol. 7, pp. 152–3). John Hoorde and Thomas Cheney, late
scholars of Eton, were also examined for the same robbery,
and confessing the fact in writing were committed to the custody
of the clerk of the check of the King's guard. Lastly, on the
14th of March—

'Nycolas Uvedale scoolemaster of Eton beyng sent for as suspect to be
counsail of a robbery lately committed at Eton by Thomas Cheney John
Horde, scolers of the sayd scole, and Gregory a servant to the sayd
scolemaster, and having certain interrogatories ministred unto hym toching
the sayd fact and other felonious trespasses wherof he was suspected did
confess that he did comitt a heinous offence with the sayd Cheney sundry
tymes hertofore and of late the vj[th] day of this present monethe in this
present yere at London : wherupon he was committed to the Marshalsey.'

In consequence of this Udall was summarily dismissed
from his mastership. Yet in spite of his confession there are
good reasons for believing that he was innocent of the graver
charges brought against him. Had they been true he would have
been ruined for life. Instead of which we find him still vicar of
Braintree in 1544, bearer of the Lord Privy Seal's letter to the
Bishop of Carlisle, then resident at Eton, and soon in high favour
at court, and associated in literary work with the Princess Mary
(Cooper, *Ralph Roister Doister*, p. xxiv). A letter is extant from
Udall to some unknown patron who has been unsuccessfully
endeavouring to procure his restitution to the mastership of Eton
(*Letters of Eminent Literary Men*, Camden Society, pp. 1–7).
From this we gather that his influential friend has 'susteined
gret travaill, peines, and trouble in that behalf,' and that Udall
wished to recover the position 'only of an honest purpose to

discharge my debtes, and by litle and litle as I might to paye every man his own.' He craves to be bestowed to 'suche condition where I maye by sobre livyng bee recovered to sum state of an honest man.' He admits that he has deserved his patron's displeasure and indignation, but trusts that his offences '*humana quidem esse et emendari posse.*' If received to grace and favour he hopes that 'this your correpcion shall bee a sufficient scourge to make me, during my lif, more wise and more ware utterly for ever to eschewe and avoid all kindes of all maner excesses and abuses that have been reported to reigne in me.' He admits that, the more tenderly his benefactor had favoured and loved him, the more grievously he must take his 'lewdnes and foly,' but he hopes for the mercy and forgiveness due 'to all suche as with wholl herte and purpose of emendemente without dissymulation returne to the holsome pathe of honestee, from whiche by youth or frailtee thei have chaunced for a tyme to swerve.' He speaks of his patron's clemency making 'of an unthrifte an honest man,' and gives examples of young men who, after being 'of a veray riottous and dissolute sorte of livynge' in youth, have become monuments 'of all frugalitee, religion, sobrietee, and holynes.' Lastly, in a sentence which seems to sum up the situation, he begs his patron to 'accepte this myn honest chaunge from vice to vertue, from prodigalitee to frugall livyng, from negligence of teachyng to assiduitee, from playe to studie, from lightness to gravitee.'

In this letter, while there is the fullest and even the most abject acknowledgement of extravagance, laxity, and neglect of duty, there is no admission of the graver offences with which he was charged.

We are confronted then with two apparently conflicting conclusions, (1) that Udall confessed his guilt before the Privy Council, (2) that he was probably innocent. How are these to be reconciled ?

If *Jacke Jugeler* was written by Udall the explanation is given in the epilogue.

In the first stanza of the epilogue we are pointedly invited to look for some ulterior significance in the play. Though the cat in the proverb had lost her eye there was some meaning in her wink ; in other words, though one cannot speak out one may hint and suggest. No tale can be told 'but that sum Englyshe maye be piked therof out,' *i.e.* some modern application may be discovered (v. note on l. 996). 'As this trifling enterlud...may signifie sum further meaning if it be well serched.' Could anything be plainer ?

It is the fashion nowadays—

> 'That the symple innosaintes ar deluded
> And an hundred thousand diuers wayes
> By suttle and craftye meanes shamefullie abused
> And by strength force and violence oft tymes compelled
> To beliue and saye the moune is made of a grene chese
> Or ells haue great harme, and parcace their life lese.'

It is an old saying that might, force, strength, power, and colourable subtlety oppress, debar, overrun and defeat right. The poor simple innocent that has had wrong and injury must call the other his 'good maister' for showing him such mercy. [Cf. such phrases in Udall's letter as, 'right worshipfull and my singlar *good Maister*' ; 'sens the tyme that your maistership, at the intercession of my good frendes, promised upon myn honest demeanure fromthensforthe to be my *good Maister*' ; 'bee *good maister* to me this .oons' ; 'I trust ye wold become *better maister* unto me.' The title 'your maistership' occurs 18 times in the letter.]

> 'And as it is daylie syne for fere of ferther disprofite
> He must that man his best frende and maister call
> Of whome he neuer receiued any maner benefite
> And at whose hand he neuer han any good at all
> And must graunt, affirme, or denie, whatsoeuer he shall
> He must saye the Croue is whight, yf he be so commaunded
> Ye and that he himselfe is into another body chaunged.'

The next stanza is still more significant if it was written by
Udall—

'He must saye he dyd amysse, though he neuer dyd offend
He must aske forgeuenes, where he did no trespace
Or ells be in troble, care and meserye without ende
And be cast in sum arrierage, without any grace
And that thing he sawe done before his owne face
He must by compulsion, stifelie denye
And for feare whether he woll or not saye tonge you lye.'

The reference to being 'cast in some arrearage' would be
explained by passages of the letter in which Udall speaks of his
'honest purpose to *discharge my debtes*,' and says that if his patron
should reject and cast him off, 'though I wer *in noo manns daunger*,
yet noo man of honor or honestee woll either receive me, or dooe
for me, or favour me, or looke on me.' Again, at the end of the
letter he says, 'where percase *aeris alieni magnitudo animum tuum
deterret* I doubte not, havyng your maistershippes favour and good
helpe, to bee hable to shake it of within two or three yeres at
the uttirmust by suche meanes as I shall declare unto your
maistership if it maye please the same to heare me.'

The epilogue continues in the same marked strain—

'He that is stronger and more of power and might
Yf he be disposed to reuenge his cause
Woll sone pike a quarell be it wronge or right
To the inferior and weker for a cople of straues
And woll agaynst him so extremelie lay the lawes
That he wol put him to the worse, other by false iniurie
Or by some craft and subtelete, or ells by plaine teranie.'

From all this we gather that some simple innocent person has
been beguiled by subtlety and forced by violence to accept and
affirm obvious impossibilities. Some influential personage has
picked a quarrel with him and ruined him by the dishonest or
arbitrary exercise of the laws. He has been compelled to call his
oppressor benefactor for sparing him, and to 'hold up his yea
and nay' even to denying his own identity. Under penalty of
endless trouble and misery, of being arrested for debt, and being

imprisoned without hope of release, he has had to confess and to ask forgiveness for an offence of which he was guiltless, to deny what he saw done before his eyes, and to give himself the lie.

May we not fairly conjecture that this is Udall's own account of the circumstances of his dismissal? It is a significant fact that his place was filled immediately by a temporary successor, and subsequently by a Mr Tyndall, whom the Bishop of Carlisle in acknowledging the letter conveyed by Udall from the Lord Privy Seal calls 'your own true scholere and bedman.' Did the Lord Privy Seal want to get Udall out in order to put his own true scholar and bedeman in? Failing to inculpate him in the alleged robbery of plate, did he, partly by threats, partly by promises of paying his debts, induce him wrongfully to confess other offences which would be enough to justify his summary dismissal? Did Udall, some seven years after, finding all these promises vain, and feeling himself strong enough in court favour to defy his oppressor, resolve in this allegorical way to repudiate his fictitious confession and rehabilitate himself in the eyes of the public?

§ 4. UDALL'S DRAMATIC WORKS. Bale, in the *Catalogus* (1557), states that Udall wrote *comoedias plures*. In the *Loseley Manuscripts* (ed. Kempe, pp. 62–3), we have a warrant dormer from Queen Mary to the 'maister and yeoman of the office of our Revells for the time being' beginning :—'Wheras our welbeloved Nicolas Udall hath at soondrie seasons convenient heretofore shewed, and myndeth hereafter to shewe, his dilligence in setting foorth of Dialogues and Enterludes before us fo' ou' regell disporte and recreacion ...we will and comaunde you...that ye deliver...to the said Udall ...out of our office of revelles, such apparell for his use as he shal thinke necessarie and requisite for the furnisshinge and condigne setting forthe of his devises before us.' This is dated 'the iii daye of Decembre, in the seconde yere of ou' reigne.'

Again (*ib.* p. 90) among extracts from accounts relating to the Office of the Revels, we find under the date X'mas, 1 and 2 Phil. and Mary, an item, 'certen plaies made by Nicholas Udall and ther incydents.' In Nichols's *Progresses of Elizabeth*, III. 177 (Cooper, *R.R.D.* p. xxxiii), under the year 1564 it is recorded that one of Udall's works was performed before Elizabeth on her visit to Cambridge :—'1564. This day (Aug. 8) was nothing done publique, save that at 9 of the clocke at night an English play called Ezekias, made by Mr Udall, and handled by King's College men only.'

§ 5. PERFORMANCE OF *Jacke Jugeler*. There are two passages in the play which enable us to fix with tolerable certainty the time of year at which *Jacke Jugeler* was performed. When the actor who took the part of Jacke Jugeler enters (vv. 84–7), he greets the audience in the following words :

> 'Our lord of Heuen and swete sainte Jhone
> Rest you merye my maisters euerychone
> And I praye to Christ and swete saint Steuen
> Send you all many a good euine.'

Again, the epilogue ends with the line :

> 'I praye god graunt, and send many a good newe yere.'

Now, as the festival of St Stephen falls on the 26th of December and that of St John on the 27th, the conclusion is irresistible that the play was written to be performed on some day or days between December 26th and 31st.

That it was written to be acted by boys is evident from vv. 75–6 :

> 'For this maker shewed vs that suche maner thinges
> Doo neuer well besime litle boyes handelinges.'

§ 6. SOURCES. The episode of Jacke Jugeler and Careawaye, vv. 331–637, is based upon the scene between Mercurius and Sosia in the *Amphitruo* of Plautus (Act I. Sc. i.), vv. 263–462 (ed. Goetz-Schoell). The dialogue between Boungrace and Careawaye, vv. 774–924, is an imitation of that between Amphitruo and Sosia (Act II. Sc. i.), vv. 551–632. The rest of the play seems to be original.

§ 7. SPELLING. The spelling of the unique copy in His Grace the Duke of Devonshire's collection shows certain marked and consistent peculiarities which prove that it belongs to an earlier edition than that represented by the two loose leaves which are contained in that copy and reproduced by the courtesy of his Grace (we believe for the first time) in the present edition. It will be noticed that the spelling of the fragment is comparatively modern and contemporary with the period at which the later edition was licensed for publication (v. § 2).

The following is a summary of the chief peculiarities of spelling in the original edition :

a > e. *emongs* (13, 258) ; *couerd* (353) ; *whilberow* (417) ; *remembrence* (729) ; *gethered* (902) ; *cheryte* (939) ; *vncomperable* (952).

a > o. *ony* (597).

e > a (before *r*). *sartayne* (171) ; *parchaunce* (297) ; *hard* (352, 598, 878, 884) ; *marcy* (471, 911) ; *marchent* (759) ; *sarue* (796) ; *sarueth* (819) ; *maruael* (825) ; *parcace* (977, 1006).

e > ea. *leasone* (100) ; *leat* (109) ; *feache* (143, 718) ; *featche* (151) ; *rekeaninges* (171) ; *geate* (356, 419) ; *heare* (481, 575) ; *neake* (577) ; *sleaping* (609) ; *cheare* (646) ; *meat* (722) ; *meaue* (826).

e > ei. *theim* (535, 641, 754).

e > i. *nides (niddes)* (17, 141, 730, 801) ; *besime* (76) ; *euine* (89) ; *reckine* (91) ; *nedithe* (97) ; *dwellith* (113) ; *cumithe* (137, 639, 689, 695) ; *maisteris* (151, 184, 202, 636) ; *gatherid* (155) ; *spokine* (190) ; *simithe* (191) ; *pice* (217) ; *simperith, prankith* (226) ; *tredith* (229) ; *quauerith, wardelith* (231) ; *wike* (274, 297) ; *spid* (276) ; *tokine* (283) ; *folowid* (286) ; *standith* (325) ; *thiues* (346) ; *beginnith* (347) ; *makith, lustith* (348) ; *spedith* (355) ; *hunderid* (358) ; *washith* (368) ; *chise* (382) ; *weighith* (383) ; *waghith* (384) ; *whilberow* (417) ; *drunkin* (441) ; *maisterlis* (479) ; *sike* (541, 860) ; *entendith* (586) ; *shakin* (592) ; *heuine* (602) ; *monethis* (651) ; *seruithe* (669) ; *disposid* (687) ; *handelid* (710, 987) ; *besiche* (732, 937) ; *bitwine* (754) ; *darist* (774) ; *knowith* (777) ; *placis* (787) ; *commaundiment* (809) ; *whither* (829) ; *dremid* (834) ; *bisiche* (871) ; *beliue* (874, 1005) ; *euin* (875) ; *speakith* (884) ; *scaterid* (901) ; *swite* (925) ; *happin* (953).

e > y. *byliue* (178) ; *my* (191, 258) ; *nyde* (194) ; *myruayllus* (259) ; *commaundyd* (260) ; *dyd (dyde)* (293, 620, 958) ; *byne* (609, 610, 709, 761, 767, 931, 932, 935) ; *lyse* (619) ; *pryue* (621) ; *byhauiore* (663) ;

handelyd (760) ; *belyue* (827) ; *euyn* (876) ; *blyssyd* (879) ; *faryd* (935) ; *bytwene* (974).

ee > i. *betwine* (119) ; *misdime* (291) ; *wine* (708) ; *thif* (746) ; *sine* (821).

i > e. *whether* (183, 628) ; *hether* (510) ; *set* (645) ; *west* (652) ; *be* (687, 723) ; *maruael* (825) ; *meserye* (1023).

i > ey. *theyther* (718).

i > ie. *fiend* (250).

o > a. *corrasiue* (657).

o > e. *yender* (256, 689) ; *buttens* (348).

o > i. *wantin* (255).

o > u. *furtune* (62) ; *cumpanie (cumpany)* (92, 859) ; *seasune* (270) ; *reasune* (271) ; *undune* (767).

u > a. *apon* (175, 566, 600, 731).

u > au. *haungrie* (380).

u > e. *tredging* (423).

u > i. *this* (751).

u > o. *loke* (180) ; *soffred* (727).

y > e. *me* (199) ; *ioylile* (725) ; *teranie* (1048).

Other peculiarities of spelling are :

scentence (65) ; *compasced* (110) ; *shurlie* (206) ; *getteth* [=*jetteth*] (226) ; *dought* (498) ; *dubtles* (637) ; *stelle* (722) ; *poumile* (725) ; *behalphe* (762) ; *calphe* (763) ; *moke* (804, 805, 812) ; *stoke* (813) ; *troiest* (822) ; *shadoo* (822-3) ; *waight* (854) ; *at tonce* (860) ; *snought* (861) ; *scacelye* (945) ; *tway* (956) ; *sertaine* (966) ; *innosaintes* (1001) ; *suttle* (1003) ; *moune* (1005) ; *whight* (1019) ; *matiers* (1038) ; *cople* (1045).

Words afterwards compounded are frequently printed apart, *e.g.*:

with in (6, 330, 344, 553) ; *with out* (28, 300, 526, 1023) ; *her of* (29) ; *who so* (45) ; *in too* (82) ; *with al* (116) ; *a late* (119) ; *albe it* (122) ; *gentle man* (124) ; *a waye* (140, 421, 601, 606, 877, 955) ; *sume what* (150, 642) ; *too morow* (197) ; *a nother* (201, 541, 627, 783, 1020) ; *after noons* (219) ; *after noone* (525) ; *a wrye* (229) ; *a non* (240, 260, 762) ; *wher vpon* (264) ; *a lone* (279) ; *a loon* (601) ; *no nother* (328) ; *a fier* (354) ; *a curste* (354) ; *me thinketh* (364) ; *a sleepe* (365) ; *a mendes* (395, 869) ; *a gayne* (461, 466, 667, 697, 956) ; *a mysse* (472, 1021) ; *a bout* (479, 569, 725) ; *a pon* (566, 731) ; *a voyde* (590) ; *here to fore* (598) ; *noo bodie* (639) ; *euery chone* (641) ; *a vou* (708) ; *a paied* (735) ; *a vise* (742) ; *straight wayes* (779) ; *vnder stood* (838) ; *a brod* (964) ; *now a dayes* (1000).

§ 8. FRAGMENT OF LATER EDITION. One leaf of the fragment corresponds to fol. D. ii. a (vv. 696–718) and to fol. D. iii. b (vv. 775–802) of the complete copy ; the other to fol. D. ii. b and D. iii. a (vv. 719–774). (See Appendix.)

The following differences of reading, other than spelling, may be noted :

Complete Copy	*Fragment*
711. 'beat me'	'beaten'
715.	omits 'misteris'
717. 'is'	'was'
718. 'was'	'wast'
723. 'But'	'By' [a misprint.]
	inserts 'first' before 'he'
724.	inserts 'present' after 'were'
725. 'wold'	'could'
726. 'drunken'	'drunck'
736. 'I knew verie well'	'this mischaunce also fel'
747. 'And I charge thee cum in my presens no more'	'And come no more in my presence'
756. 'haue with me parte'	'with me haue part'
758. (head-line) 'Jacke iugler'	'Jugler'
764. 'angered'	'an angred'
768. 'But now I haue reuenged my quarell'	'Wel, sith that now reuenged is my quarel'
769.	omits 'this'
774. 'darist'	'dare'
776.	inserts 'you' after 'tolde'
777. 'folkes knowith'	'folke knowe'
784. (head-line) 'Boungrace'	'Maister Boungrace'
789. 'I shreue'	'Beshrew'
798. (head-line) 'Boungrace'	'Maister Boungrace'
802. 'said'	'saydst'

From this it is evident that the fragment represents a careful revision of the original edition so as to bring it up to modern requirements in the matters of punctuation, spelling, grammar and metre. The punctuation has been corrected, but an unfortunate convention has been adopted, by which a colon has been put at the end of the first line of each couplet and a full stop at the end of the second, without reference to the sense. Constructions that had become archaic have been modernised, *e.g.* ' was thou ' becomes ' wast thou ' ; 'thou said' becomes 'thou saydst.' The metre has been normalised by changing the order of the words, or by the addition or omission of expletives. These are all printer's corrections, and merely imply that the original copy was carefully ' edited ' for later publication.

§ 9. MODERN EDITIONS. In 1820 *The Interludes of Jack Jugler and Thersytes* were edited for the Roxburghe Club by Joseph Haslewood. *Jacke Jugeler* was included in *Four Old Plays* (ed. Child, 1848), and in Hazlitt's edition of Dodsley's *Old English Plays* (1874). Dr Grosart reprinted it directly from the original, adding an introduction and notes, in vol. IV of his *Miscellanies of the Fuller Worthies Library* (printed for private circulation, 1872–1876).

The editor desires to acknowledge his obligation to the Duke of Devonshire for permission to photograph the pages of the unique original in the Chatsworth Library ; to the late Duke of Devonshire for similar courtesy in respect of the two loose leaves of another edition, contained in the unique copy and here reproduced as an appendix ; also to Mrs S. Arthur Strong, formerly Librarian and Keeper of the Duke of Devonshire's Collections, for taking the two leaves to Oxford to be photographed at the Clarendon Press ; also to Professor E. Bensly for extracts from Arber's *Transcript of the Stationers' Register*, and to Professor Bang for the suggestion that *Jacke Jugeler* was written by Nicholas Udall.

Irregular, Doubtful and Erroneous Readings.

The following are the readings of the original edition :

25. industruis
    lnstie
28. with out
41. Ppilosophers
104. yers ?
105. yon
148. prceious
171. Sartayde
207. sumpretie
217. gingerlte
228. Se
231. wardelith
239. tael
310. stoding
427. lynes
438. Caerawaye
452. thyne ?
464. Careawaye (misplaced)
465. chaung
466. see (thee ?)
481. y^e (y^t ?)
486. one
    thy
490. cae (contraction of Care-
    awaye ?)

494. iacke iugler (misplaced)
515. y^e (y^t ?)
527. Aud
590. slinking
658. maisterishps
713. lytle (broken t)
735. full (broken f)
742. bete (broken t)
777. I (inverted)
798. knane
825. maruael
861. knanes
870. befound
878. a other
925. swite
934. hane
968. waister
985. I
997. yfso
1005. aud
1044. wollsone
1060. gidaū

ꙮ A new Enterlued for

Chyldren to playe, named Jacke Jugeler, both wytte, and very playsent. Newly Imprented.

❧ The Players names.

Mayster Boungrace	A galant
Dame cope	A Gentelwoman
Jacke Jugler	The vyce
Jenkin careaway	A Lackey.
Ales trype and go	A mayd.

Bougrace.

Jacke Jugler.

✻ THE PROLOGUE

INterpone tuis interdum gaudia curis
  Ut possis animo quemues sufferre laborem
Doo any of you knowe what latine is this
Or ells wold you haue, an expositorem
To declare it in Englyshe, per sensum planiorem   5
It is best I speake Englyshe, or ells with in a whylle
I may percace myne owne selfe, with my latin begile.

The two verses, which I rehersid before
I finde written, in the boke of Cato the wyse
Emongs good precepts, of lyuing a thousand more   10
Which to folowe there, he doth all men auise
And they may be Englyshed, breflie in this wyse
Emongs thy carful busines, vse sume time mirth and ioye
That no bodilye worke, thy wyttes breke or noye.

For the mynd (saith he) in serious matters occupied   15
Yf it haue not sum quiet mirthe, and recreacion
Interchaungeable admixed, must niddes be sone weried
And (as who should saye) tried, through continual operacion
Of labour and busines, without relaxacion
Therfore intermix honest mirthe, in suche wise   20
That your streght may be refreshid, and to labours suffise

For as meat and drinke, naturall rest and slepe
For the conseruacion, and helth of the bodye
Must niddes be had, soo the mynd and wittes to kepe
Pregnant, freshe industruis, quike and lnstie 25
Honest mirthe, and pastime, is requisite and necessarie
For, Quod caret alterna requie durabile non est
Nothing may endure (saith Ouyd) with out sum rest.

Example, proufe her of in erth is well founde
Manifest open and verie euident 30
For except the husbandman suffer his grounde
Sum tymes to rest, it wol bere no frute verament
Therfore they lett the filde lye, euerie second yeare
To the end that after rest, it may the better corne beare.

Thus than (as I haue sayed) it is a thyng naturall 35
And naturallie belonging to all lyuing creatures
And vnto man especiallie, aboue others all
To haue at times coueniĕt pastaŭce, mirthe, and pleasurs
So thei be ioyned wt honestie, and keapt wt in due measurs
And the same well allowed not onlye the said Cato 40
But also ye Ppilosophers, Plutarke, Socrates and Plato

And Cicero Tullius, a man sapient and wyse
Willeth the same, in that his fyrst boke
Which he wrot, and entytulid, of an honest mans office
Who so is disposid therupon to looke 45
Wher to define, and offirme, he boldlie on him tooke
That to here Enterluds, is pastime conuenient
For all maner men, and a thing congruent.

He rekeneth that namelie, as a verie honest disport
And aboue al other thinges, commendeth ye old cōmedie 50
The hearing of which, may doo the mynd cumfort
For they be replenished with precepts of Philosophie
The conteine mutch wisdome and teache prudēt pollecie
and though thei be al writē of mattiers of non ɪportaūce
Yet the shew great wit, and mutch pretie conueiaunce.   55

And in this maner of making, Plautus did excell
As recordeth the same Tullius cōmending him bi name
Wherfore this maker deliteth passinglye well
Too folowe his argumentes, and drawe out the same
For to make at seasuns cōueniēt pastims mirth and game 60
As now he hath dō this matter not worth an oyster shel
Except percace it shall furtune too make you laugh well

And for that purpose onlye this maker did it write
Taking the ground therof out of Plautus first cōmedie
And the first scentence of ye same for higher things endite 65
In no wise he wold, for yet the time is so quesie
That he that speaketh best, is lest thanke worthie
Therfore, sith noting but trifles maye be had
you shal here a thing yt onlie shal make you merie and glad.

And suche a trifling matter as when it shalbe done   70
Ye may report and saye ye haue hearde nothing at all
Therfore I tell you all, before it be begone
That noman looke to heare of matters substancyall
Nor mattiers of any grauitee either great or small
For this maker shewed vs that suche maner thinges   75
Doo neuer well besime litle boyes handelinges.

Wherfore yf ye wyl not sowrelie your broues bende
At suche a fantasticall conceite as this
But can be content to heare and see the ende
I woll go shew the Players what your pleasure is   80
Which to wait vpon you I know bee redie or this
I woll goo sende them hither in too your presence
Desiryng that they may haue quiet audience.

✻ Jake Jugler

OUr lord of Heuen and swete sainte Jhone
Rest you merye my maisters euerychone   85
And I praye to Christ and swete saint Steuen
Send you all many a good euine
And you to syr, and you, and you also
Good euine to you an hundered times and a thousand mo
Now by all thes crosses of fleshe bone and blod   90
I reckine my chaunce right maruaylus good
Here now to find all this cumpanie
Which in my mynde I wyshed for hartylie
For I haue labored all daye tyll I am werie
And now am disposed too passe the time, and be merie   95
And I thinke noon of you, but he wolde do the same
For who wol be sad, and nedithe not, is foule to blame
And as for mee, of my mother I haue byn tought
To bee merie when I may, and take no thought
Which leasone, I bare so well awaye   100
That I vse to make merye oons a daye
And now if all thinges happyn right
You shall see as mad a pastime this night

As you saw this seuen yers ? and as propre a toye
As euer yon saw played of a boye   105
I am called Jake Jugler, of many an oon
And in faith I woll playe a iugling cast a non
I woll cunger the moull, and god before
Or elles leat me lese my name for euer more
I haue it deuised, and compasced hou   110
And what wayes, I woll tell and shew to you
you all know well Maister Boungrace
The gentilman that dwellith here in this place
And Jenkine Carreawaie, his page as cursed a lad
And as vngracious as euer man had   115
An vnhappy wage, and as folishe a knaue with al
As any is now, within London wall
This Jenkine and I been fallen at great debate
For a mattier, that fell betwine vs a late
And hitherto of him I could neuer reuenged be   120
For his maister mantaineth hī, and loueth not me
Albe it the very truth to tell
Nother of thē both, knoweth me not verie well
But against al other boies, the sayd gentle man
Maynteyneth him, all that he can   125
But I shall set lytle by my wyte
If I do not Jenkine this night requite
Ere I slepe Jenkine shall bee mete
And I trust to cume partlye out of his dete
And whan we mete againe, if this do not suffise   130
I shall paye Jenkine the residue, in my best wyse
It chaūced me right now in the other end of ye next stret
With Jenkine and his mayster, in the face to met

I aboed ther a whylle, playng for to see
At the Buklers, as welbecommed mee   135
It was not longe tyme, but at the last
Bake cumithe my cosune Careawaie, homward ful fast
Pricking, Praunsing, and springynge in his short cote
And pleasauntlie synginge, with a mery note
Whyther a waye so fast, tary a whyle sayed oon   140
I cannot now sayd Jenkine, I must nides bee goon
My maister suppeth herbye, at a gentylmans place
And I must thither feache my dame, maistres bougrace
But yet er I go, I care not motche
At the bukelers to playe, with thee oon faire toche   145
To it they went, and played so long
Tyll Jenkine thought he had wrong
By cokes prceious potstike, I wyll not home this night
Quod he, but as good a stripe oon thie hed lyght
Within halfe an houre, or sume what lese   150
Jenkine lefte playng, and went to featche his maisteris
But by the waye he met with a Freuteres wyfe
There Jenkine and she fell at suche strife
For snatching of an Apple, that doune he cast
Her basket, and gatherid vp the apples fast   155
And put them in his sleue, thē came he his waye
By an other lane, as fast as he maye
tyll he came at a corner, by a shoops stall
Where boyes were at Dice, faryng at all
When Careawaie with that good cumpany met   160
He fell to faryng, withouten let
Forgettyng his message, and so well did he fare
that whan I came bye, he gan swere and stare

And full bitterlye, began to curse
As oone that had lost, almost all in his purse   165
For I knowe his olde gise, and condicion
Neuer to leaue, tyll all his mony bee goon
For he hath noo mony, but what he doth stell
And that woll he playe, awaye euery dell
I passed by, and then called vnto my mynd   170
Sartayde old rekeaninges, that were behynd
Bitwen Jenkine and me, whõ partlie to recõpence
I trust by gods grace, ere I goo hence
This garments, cape, and all other geare
That now you see, apon me here   175
I haue doon oon, all lyke vnto his
For the nons, and my purpose is
To make Jenkine, byliue yf I can
That he is not him selfe, but an other man
For except he hath better loke, than he had   180
He woll cum hyther, starke staryng mad
Whan he shall cum, I wol handle my captine so
That he shal not well wot, whether too goo
His Maisteris I know, she woll him blame
And his Mayster also, wyll doo the same   185
Because that she, of her supper deceiued is
For I am sure they haue all supped by this
But and if Jenkine, wold hither resort
I trust he and I, should make sum sport
Yf I had sooner spokine, he wold haue sooner been here   190
For my simithe, I do his voyce heare.

¶ Careawaye

A syr I may saye, I haue been at a fest
I haue lost .ii.s. and syxpence at the lest
Mary syr, of this gaynes I nyde make no bost
But the dyuell goo with all, more haue I lost   195
My name is Careawaie, let all sorow passe
I woll ere too morow night be as rich as euer I was
Or at ye forthest within a day or twaine
Me Maysters purse, shall paye me agayne
Therfor hogh careawaie, now wol I sĩg. hei hei   200
But bi ye lorde now I remembre a nother thing
By my faith Jenkine my Maisteris and thou
Ar lyke to gree, god knoweth hou
That thou comest not, for her incontinent
To bryng hir to supper, when thou were sent   205
And now they haue all supped, thou wolt shurlie abye
Except thou imagine, sumpretie and craftye lye
For she is as all other weomen bee
A verie cursed shrew, by the blessid Trinitie
And a verye Dyuell, for yf she oons begyne   210
To fyght, or chyde, in a weke she wol not lyne
And a great pleasure she hath, specyally now of late
To gette poore me, now and then by the pate
For she is an angrye pece of fleshe, and sone displeasyd
Quikely moued, but not lyghtlye appesed   215
We vse to call her at home, dame Coye
A pretie gingerlie pice, god saue her and saint Loye
As denty and nice, as an halpeny worth of siluer spoons
But vengable melancolie, in the after noons
She vseth for hir bodylie helth, and safegard   220

To chyd daylie oone fite, too supperward
And my Mayster him selfe, is worse then she
If he ons throughlye angeryd bee
And a mayd we haue at home, Aulsoon tripe and goo
Not all London can shewe, suche other twoo   225
She simperith, she prankith and getteth with out faylle
As a pecocke that hath spred, and sheweth hir gaye taile
Se minceth, she brideleth, she swimmeth to and fro
She tredith not one here a wrye, she tryppeth like a do
Abrode in the strete, going or cumming homward   230
She quauerith, and wardelith, like one in a galiard
Euerye ioynt in her bodye and euerie part
Oh it is a ioylie wenche to myns and deuyd a fart
She talketh, she chatteth like a Pye all daye
And speaketh like a parat Poppagaye   235
And that as fine, as a small silken threede
Ye and as high as an Eagle can fle for a neade
But it is a spitfull lying girle, and neuer well
But whan she may sum yll tael by me tel
She woll I warrant you, a non at the first   240
Of me immagine, and saye the worst,
And what soeuer she to my maisteris doth saye
It is writen in the gosspell of the same daye
Therfore I woll here with my selfe deuise
What I may best say, and in what wise   245
I may excuse this my long taryeng
That she of my negligence may suspect nothyng
For if the faulte of this be found in mee
I may giue my life for halpenis three
    Hic cogitabundo similis sedeat.

Let me stodie this moneth, and I shall not fiend 250
A better deuise then now is cume to my mynd
Maistries woll I saye, I am bound by my dutie
To see that your womanhod haue no iniurie
For I heare and see, more then you now and then
And your selfe partlie know the wantin wyles of men 255
When wee came yender, there dyd I see
My mayster kisse gentilwomen tow or three
And to come emongs others my thought bysye
He had a myruayllus great phantasye
A non he commaundyd me to run thens for you 260
To cume supe there if you wold but I wot not how
My hart grudgid mistrusting lest that I being awaye
My maister wold sum light cast playe
Wher vpon maistries, to se the ende
I tarried halfe supper time so god me mende 265
And besydes that there was such other compainye
As I know your maistrisship setteth nothing by
Gorges dames of the corte and galaunts also
With doctours, and other rufflers mo
At last whan I thought it tyme and seasune 270
I cam too certifie you as it was reasune
And by the way whome should I mete
But that most honest Gentilman in the stret
Which the last wike was with you here
And made you a banket, and bouncing cheare 275
Ah Jenkin quoth he good spid how farest thou
Mary wel god yld it you maister quoth I how do you
How dothe thy maisteris is she at home
Ye syr quoth I and suppeth all alone

And but she hath noo maner good chere   280
I am sure she wold gladlye haue you there
I cannot cum now sayd he I haue busines
But thou shalt carie a tokine from me to thy maistreis
Goo with me too my chaumbre at yone lane end
And I woll a dishe of costerds vnto hyr send   285
I folowid him, and was bolde by your leaue
To receiue and bring them here in my sleue
But I wold not for all Englond by Jhesu Chryst
That my maister Boungrace herof wyst
Or knew that I should any such geare to you bring   290
Lest he misdime vs both in sum worse thyng
Nor shew him nothyng of that I before sayed
For then in dyd syr I am arayed
Yf you doo I may nothing herafter vnto you tell
whether I se mi master doo ill or well   295
That if you now this counsaile kepe
I wol ease you parchaunce twise in a wike
you may saye you wer sike and your hed did ake
that you lusted not this night any supper make
Speciallye with out the dores but thought it best   300
too abyde at home and take your rest
And I wyll to my maister too bryng hym home
For you know he wolbe angrie if he come alone
this woll I saye and face it so well
That she shall beleue it euerye dell   305
Hou saye you frinds, by the armes of Robyn hood
Wol not this excuse be resonable good
To muse for any better, great foly it is
For I may make sure rekenning of this

That and if I wold sit stoding this .vii. yere   310
I shall not ells find how to saue me all clere
And as you see for the most part our witts be best
When wee be takyne most vnrediest
But I wol not giue for that boye a flye
That hath not al tymes in store one good lye   315
And cannot set a good face vpon the same
Therfore saint Gorge ye boroue, as it wol let him frame
I woll ieopard a ioynt, bee as bee maye
I haue had many lyke chaunces, before this daye
But I promise you I do curstlie feare   320
For I feel a vengeable burning in my left ere
And it hath byn a saying, of tyme long
That swete mete woll haue soure sauce among
And surelye I shall haue sum ill hape
For my here standith vp vnder my cape   325
I would knocke but I dare not by our ladye
I feare hanging where vnto no man is hastie
But seing there is no nother remedie
Thus to stand any longer it is but folye.
                    Hic pulset ostium.
They bee soo farre with in, the cannot heare   330

ℂ Jacke Jugler

Soft thy knoking saucie knaue, what makest thou there

Jenkene Careawaie

What knaue is that ? he speaketh not too me I trowe
And we mete the one of vs is lyke to haue a blowe
For nowe that I am well chafed, and sumwhat hote

twentye suche could I hewe as small as fleshe to pote   335
And surelie if I had a knyfe
This knaue should escape hardelye with his lyfe
To teache him to aske of me any more
What I make at my owne maistirs doore

ℂ Jacke Jugler

But if thou come from that gate thou knaue   340
I woll fet thee by the swet lookes so god me saue

❋ Jenkine Careawaie

Woll the horesoon fyght in dede by myn honestie
I know no quarell he hath too me
But I wold I were with in the house
And then I wold not set by hym a louse   345
For I feare and mistrust suche quareling thiues
See how he beginnith to strike vp his sleues

ℂ Jacke iugler

His arse makith buttens now, and who lustith to feale
Shall find his hart creping out at his heele
Or ells lying hiden in sum corner of his hose   350
Yf it be not alredie dropped out of his nose
For as I doubt not but you haue hard beforne
A more dastard couerd knaue was neuer borne

❋ Jenkin Careawaie

The diuell set the house a fier, I trowe it is a curste
When a man hath most hast he spedith worst   355
Yf I bee robed, or slayne, or any harme geate

The fault is in them that dothe not me in lete
And I durst ieoperd, an hunderid pounde
That sum bauderie might now within be founde
But except sum of them come the soner   360
I shall knocke suche a peale, that al englond shal wŏder

❡ Jake iugler

Knoke at the gate hardelye agayne if thou dare
And seing thou wolt not bye faire words beware
Now fistes, me thinketh yesterdaye .vii. yers past
That four men a sleepe at my fete you cast   365
And this same day you dyd no maner good
Nor were not washen in warme blod

❀ Jenkin Careawaie

What whorson is this that washith in warme blod
Sum diuell broken loose, out of hell for wood
Four hath he slayne, and now well I see   370
That it must be my chaunce the fift to bee
But rather then thus shamfullye too be slayne
wold Christ my frends had hanged me being but yers .ii
And yet if I take good hart and be bolde
Percace he wolbe more sobre and coulde   375

❡ Jake iugler

Now handes bestur you about his lyppes and face
And streake out all his teth without any grace
Gentelman are you disposed to eate any fist mete

❀ Jenkin Careawaye

I haue supped I thanke you syr and lyst not to eate
Geue it to them that are haungrie if you be wyse   380

❡ Jacke iugler

Yet shall do a man of your dyet no harme to suppe twise
This shalbe your Chise, to make your met digest
For I tell you thes handes weighith of the best

✻ Jenkin Careawaye

I shall neuer escape see how he waghith his handes

❡ Jacke iugler

with a stroke they wyll lay a knaue in our ladye boons   385
And this day yet they haue done no good at all

✻ Jenkine Careawaye

Ere ye assaye thē on mee, I praie thee lame thē on ye wal
But speake you all this in earnest, or in game
Yf you be angrie with me trulye you are to blame
For haue you any iust quarell to mee   390

❡ Jake iugler

Eer thou and I parte that wol I shew thee

✻ Jenkin Careawaye

Or haue I doone you any maner displeasure

❡ Jake iugler

Ere thou and I parte thou shalt know, ye maist besure

✻ Jenkin Careawaye

By my faith yf thou be angrie without a cause
You shall haue a mendes made with a cople of straus   395
By thee I sette what soeuer thou arte
But for thy displeasure I care not a farte
May a man demaund whose seruant you bee

¶ Jacke iugler

My maisters seruaunt I am for veritie

❋ Jenkin Careawaye

what busynes haue you at thys place now 400

Jacke iugler

Nay mary tell me what busynes hast thou
For I am commaunded for to watche and giue diligence
That in my good maister Boungraces absence
Noo misfortune may happen to his house sertayne

❋ Jenkin Careawaye

well now I am cume, you may go hens agayne 405
And thanke them yt somuch for my maister hath doone
Sewing them yt the seruants of yr house be cume home
For I am of the house, and now in woll I goo

¶ Jacke iugler

I cannot tell whether thou be of the house or noo
But goo no nere, lest I handle thee like a strainger 410
Thanke no man but thy selfe, if thou be in any daunger

¶ Jenkine Careawaye

Marye I defye thee, and planly vnto thee tell
That I am a seruaunt of this house, and here I dwell

Jacke iugler

Now soo god me snache, but thou goo thee waies
Whille thou mayest, for this fortie dayes 415
I shall make thee not able to goo nor ryde
But in a dungcart or a whilberow liyng on on syde

❡ Jenken Careawaie

I am a seruaunt of this house by thes .x. bons

�֍ Jacke iugler

Noo more prating but geat thee hens at towns

Jenkin Careawaye

Why my mayster hath sent me home in his message		420

�֍ Jacke iugler

Pike and walke a knaue, here a waye is no passage

❡ Jenkin Careawaie

What wilt thou let me from my nowne maistirs house

✖ Jacke iugler

Be tredging, or in faith you bere me a souse
Here my mayster and I haue our habitacion
And hath continually dwelled in this mansyon		425
At the least this doosen yers and od
And here wol we end our lyues by the grace of god

❡ Jenkin Careawaye

Why then where shall my maister and I dwell

✖ Jacke iugler

At the Dyuell yf you lust, I can not tell

❡ Jenken Careawaye

In nomine patris, now this geare doth passe		430
For a litel before supper here our house was
And this day in ye morning I wol on a boke swer
That my maister and I both dwelleyd here

☙ Jake iugler

Who is thy mayster tell me with out lye
And thine owne name also let me knowe shortlie   435
For my maysters all, let me haue the blame
Yf this knaue kno his master or his owne name

❀ Caerawaye

My maisters name is maister Boungrace
I haue dwelled with him a longe space
And I am ienkin Careawaye his page   440

☙ Jake iugler

What ye drunkin knaue begin you to rage
Take that, art thou maister Boungracis page

❀ Careawaie

Yf I be not, I haue made a verye good viage

☙ Jacke iugler

Darest thou too my face saye thou art I

❀ Careawaye

I wolde it were true and no lye   445
For then thou sholdest smart, and I should bet
Where as now I do all the blowes get

☙ Jacke iugler

And is maister Boungrace thy maister doest ye then saye

❀ Careawaye

I woll swere on a booke, he was ons this daye

❡ Jacke iugler

And for that thou shalt sumwhat haue   450
Because thou presumest, like a saucye lying knaue
To saye my maister is thyne ? who is thy maister now ?

✻ Careawaie

By my trouthe syr who so euer please you
I am your owne, for you bete me soo
As no man but my mayster sholde doo   455

Jake iugler

I woll handle thee better if faut be not in fyst

Careawaie

Helpe saue my life maisters for ye passion of christ

Jacke iugler

Why thou lowsy thefe doest thou crye and rore

Careawaye

No fayth I woll not crye one whit more
Saue my lyfe helpe, or I am slaine   460

Jacke iugler

Ye doest thou make a romeringe yet a gayne
Dyd not I byde the holde thy peace

✻ Careawaie

In faith now I leaue crieng, now I sease helpe, helpe,

❡ Jacke iugler

Who is thy maister   Careawaye
Mayster Boungrace

¶ Jacke iugler

I woll make the chaung yt song, ere wee pas this place 465
For he is my maister, and a gaine to see I saye
That I am his ienkin Careawaye
Who art thou now tell me plaine

❋ Careawaye

Noo bodye, but whome please you sertayne

Jacke iugler

Thou saydest euen now thy name was Careawaie 470

❋ Careawaye

I crye you marcy syr, and forgiuenes praye
I said a mysse because it was soo too daye
And thought it should haue continued alwaies
Like a fole as I am and a dronken knaue
But in faith syr yee se all the wytte I haue 475
Therfore I beseche you do me no more blame
But giue me a new maister, and an other name
For it wold greue my hart soo helpe me god
To runne about the stretes like a maisterlis nod

¶ Jake iugler

I am he that thou saydest thou were 480
And maister boungrace is my maister ye dweleth heare
thou art no poynt Careawaye thi witts do thee faylle

❋ Careawaye

Ye mary syr you haue bette them doune into my taylle
But syr myght I be bolde to saye on thyng
Without any bloues, and without any beatynge 485

℃ Jake iugler

Truce for a whyle say one what thy lust

Careawaye

May a man too your honeste by your woord trust
I pray you swere by the masse you woll do me no yll

℃ iacke iugler

By my faith 1 promise pardone thee I woll

Careawaye

What and you kepe no promise. Ja iugler, then vpŏ cae   490
I praie god light as much or more as hath on ye to daye

Careawaye

Now dare I speake so mote I thee
Maister boungrace is my maister, and the name of mee
is ienken careaway, iacke iugler.   What saiest thou soo
careawaye
And yf thou wilt strike me, and breake thy promise, doo   495
And beate on mee, tyll I stinke, and tyll I dye
And yet woll I still saye that I am I

℃ iacke iugler

This bedlem knaue without dought is mad

℃ Careawaye

No by god for all that I am a wyse lad
And can cale to rememberaunce euery thynge   500
That 1 dyd this daye, sithe my vprisynge
For went not I wyth my mayster to daye
Erly in the morning to the Tenis playe ?

At noone whyle my maister at his dynner sate
Played not I at Dice at the gentylmans gate 505
Did not I wayte on my maister to supperward
And I thĩke I was not chaũged ye way hõward
Or ells if thou thinke I lye
Aske in the stret of them that I came bye
And sith that I cam hether into your presens 510
what man lyuing could carye me hens
I remember I was sent to fetche my maisteris
And what I deuised to saue me harmeles
Doo not I speake now is not this my hande
Be not these my feet ye on this ground stand ? 515
Did not this other knaue her knoke me about ye hede ?
And beat me tyll I was almost dede ?
How may it then bee, that he should bee I ?
Or I not my selfe it is a shamfull lye
I woll home to our house, whosoeuer say naye 520
For surelye my name is ienkin Careawaye

⁊ Jacke Jugler

I wol make thee say otherwise ere we depart if we can

⁊ Jenkin Careawaye

Nay that woll I not in faith for no man
Except thou tell me what I thou hast doone
Euer syth fiue of the cloke this after noone 525
Reherse me all that with out anye lye
Aud then I woll confesse that thou art I

❋ Jacke iugler

When my maister came to the gentylmãs place
He cõmaunded me too rune home a great pace

Too fet thyther my maisteris and by the waye   530
I dyd a good whyle at the bukelers playe
Then came I by a wife that did costerds sell
And cast downe hir basket fayre and well
And gathered as many as I could gete
And put theim in my sleue here they bee yet   535

⟡ Careawaie

How the diuell should they cume there
For I dyd them all in my owne sleue bere
He lyeth not a worde in all this
Nor dothe in any one poynt myse
For ought I se yet betwene erneste and game   540
I must go sike me a nother name
But thou mightest see al this, tel the rest that is behind
And there I know I shal thee a lyer fynd

✳ Jacke iugler

I ran thence homeward a contrarye waye
And whether I stoped there or naye   545
I could tell if me lusteth a good token
But it may not very well be spoken

Jenkin Careawaye

Noo may I praye thee let no man that here
But tell it me priuelye in mine ere

✳ Jacke iugler

I thou lost all thy mony at dice christ geue it his curse   550
wel and truelye pycked before out of an other mãs porse

℃ Jenken Careawaie

Godes bodye horeson thefe who tolde thee that same
Sum cunning diuell is with in thee payne of shame
In nomine patris, god and our blessed ladye
Now and euermore saue me from thy cumpanye   555

℃ Jacke iugler

How now art thou Careawaye or not

�֍ Careawaye

By the lorde I doubte, but sayest thou nay to that

Jacke iugler

Ye mary I tell thee care awaye is my name

℃ Careawaye

And by these tene bones myne is the same
Or ells tell me yf I be not hee   560
What my name frome hensforth shall bee

✖ iacke iugler

By my fayth the same that it was before
Whan I lust too be Careawaye no more
Looke well vpon me, and thou shalt see as now
That I am ienkyne Careawaye and not thou   565
Looke well a pon me, and by euerye thyng
Thou shalt well know that I make no leasing.

Careawaye

I se it is soo without any doubte
But how the dyuell came it a boute
Who soo in England lokethe on him stedelye   570
Sall perceiue plainlye that he is I

I haue sene my selfe a thousand times in a glasse
But soo lyke my selfe as he is neuer was
He hath in euerye poynt my clothing and mi geare
My hed, my cape, my shirt and notted heare   575
And of the same coloure, my yes, nose and lyppes
My chekes chine, neake, feete, leges, and hippes
Of the same stature, and hyght and age
And is in euery poynt maister Boungrace page
That if he haue a hole in his tayle   580
He is euen I myne owne selfe without any faile
And yet when I remembre I wot not how
The same mā yt I haue euer bine me thinkith I am now
I know mi maister, and his house, and my fiue witts I haue
Why then should I giue credence to this folishe knaue   585
That nothing entendith but me delude and mooke
For whom should I feare at my masters gate to knoke

Jacke iugler

Thinkest thou I haue sayde all this in game
Goo or I shall send the hens in the dyuills name
A voyde thou lousye lurden and precious slinking slaue   590
that nether thi name knowest nor canst ani maister haue
wine shakin, pilorye pecpours, of lice not wtout a pecke
Hens or by gods precious I shall breake thy necke

ⓒ Careawaye

Then mayster I besiche you hartylye take the payne
Yf I be found in any place too bringe me to me againe   595
Now is not this a wonderfull case
That no man should lease him selfe soo in ony place

Haue any of you harde of suche a thyng here to fore
No nor neuer shall I dare saie from hensforth any more

℃ Jacke iugler

Whyle he museth an iudgeth him selfe apon   600
I woll stele a waye for a whyle and let him a loon

✻ Careawaie

Good lorde of heuine, where dyd I my selfe leaue
Or who did me of my name by the waye bereue
For I am sure of this in my mynde
That I dyd in no place leue my selfe byhinde   605
Yf I had my name played a waye at dyce
Or had sold my selfe to any man at a pryce
Or had made a fray and had lost it in fyghtyng
Or it had byne stolne from me sleaping
It had byne a matter and I wold haue kept pacience   610
But it spiteth my hart to haue lost it by suche open negligence
Ah thou horesone drousie drunken sote
Yt were an almes dyde to walke thy cote
And I shrew him that wold for thee be sorye
Too see thee well curryed by and by   615
And by Chryst if any man wold it doo
I my selfe wold helpe there too
For a man may see thou horesone goose
Thou woldest lyse thyne arse if it were loose
Albeit I wolde neuer the dyde beleue   620
But that the thing it selfe doth shewe and pryue
There was neuer Ape so lyke vnto an Ape
As he is to me in feature, and shape

But what woll my maister say trow ye
When he shall this geare here and see   625
Wyl he know me thinke you, when he shal se me
Yf he do not a nother woll as good as he
But where is that other I ? whether is he gon
To my mayster by cockes precius passion
Eyther to put me out of my place   630
Or too accuse me to my maister Boungrace
But I woll after as fast as I can flee
I trust to be there as soone as hee
That yf my mayster be not redye home to come
I woll be here agayne as fast as I can rune   635
In any wyse to speake with my maysteris
Or ells I shall neuer escape hanging dubtles

Dame Coye

I shall not sup̄pe this night full wel I see
For as yet noo bodie cumithe for to fet mee
But good ynough let me alone   640
I woll bee euen with theim euery chone
I saye nothing, but I thinke sum what I wis
Sum ther bee that shall here of this
Of al vnkind and churlishe husbands this is ye cast
To let ther wyues set at home and fast   645
While they bee forth and make good cheare
Pastime, and sporte, as now he doth there
But yf I were a wyse woman, as I am a mome
I shold make my selfe as good chere at home
But if he haue thus vnkindlye serued mee   650
I woll not forget it this monethis three

And if I west ye fault were in him, I pray god I be ded
But he shoulde haue suche a kyrie, ere he went too bed
As he neuer had before in all his lyfe
Nor any man ells haue had of his wyfe   655
I wolde rate him and shake him after such a sorte
As sholde be to him a corrasiue, full lytle to his cumforte

Alis trippe and goo
Yf I may be so bolde by your maisterishps lycens
As too speake and shew my mynde and sentence
I thinke of this you may the boye thanke   660
For I know that he playeth you many a lyke pranke
And that wolde you saye, yf you knew as mutch as wee
That his daylye conuersacion and byhauiore see
For yf you commaund him to goo speake with sum one
Yt is an houre ere he wolbe gone   665
Then woll he rune forth, and playe in the strete
And cume a gaine and say that he cannot with him mete

Dame Coye
Naye, naye, it is his maisters playe
He seruithe me soo almost euerye third daye
But I wolbe euen with him as god geue me ioy   670
And yet the fault may bee in the boye
As vngracious a graft so mot I thriue
As any goeth on goddes ground a lyue

Careawaye
My witte is breched in suche a brake
That I cannot deuise what way is best to take   675
I was almost as fare as my maister is
But then I begane to remember this

And to cast the worst as on in fere
yf he chaunce to see mee and kepe me there
Til he cum him selfe, and speake with mi masteris   680
Then am I lyke to bee in shrewd dystres
yet were I better thought I to turne hom again
And fyrst speake with her certayne
Cockes bodie yonder she standeth at the dore
Now is it wourse then it was before   685
Wold christ I could get againe out of hir sight
For I see be her looke she is disposid to fyght
Bi ye lord she hath ther an angrie shrewes loke

Dame coye

Loe yender cumithe that vnhappye hooke

❊ Careawaye

God saue you maysteris doo you know me well   690

Dame coye

Cume nere hither vnto mee, and I shall thee tell
Why thou noughtie vyllan is that thy gyse
To gest with thy maisteris in suche wise
take that to begyne with, and god before
When thy maister cumith home thou shalt haue more   695
For he told me when he forth wente
That thou shouldest cume bake a gaine incontinente
To brynge me to supper where he now is
And thou hast plaid by the waie, and thei haue don bi this
But no force I shall thou mayst trust mee   700
Teache all naughtie knaues to beware by thee

✳ Careawaye

For sothe maisteris yf you knew as much as I
ye woulde not be with me halfe so angrie
For the faulte is neither in mi maister nor in me nor you
But in an other knaue that was here euen now   705
And his name was ienkin Careawaie

Dame coye

What I see my man is disposid to playe
I wine he be dronken or mad I make god a vou

❦ Careawaie

Nay I haue byn made sobre and tame I now
I was neuer so handelid before in all my lyfe   710
I would euery man in England had so beat me his wife
I haue forgotten with tousing by the here
What I deuised to say a lytle ere

Dame coye

Haue I lost my supper this night through thi negligēce

❦ Careawaye

Nay then wer I a knaue misteris, sauing your reuerēce   715

Dame coye

Why I am sure that by this time it is doone

✳ Careawaye

Ye that it is more then an our agone

Dame coye

And was not thou sent to feache mee theyther

Careawaye

Yes and had cume right quiklie hither
But that by the waye I had a gret fall   720
And my name, body shape legges and all
And meat with one, that from me did it stelle
But be god he and I sum bloues dyd deale
I wolde he were now before your gate
For you wold poumile him ioylile a bout the pate   725

Dame Coye

Truelye this wagepastie is either drunken or mad

� Careawaye

Neuer man soffred so mutche wrong as I had
But maisteris I should saye a thinge to you
Tary it wol cum to my remembrence euen now
I must niddes vse a substanciall premeditacion   730
For the matter lyeth gretylie me a pon
I besiche your maisterishipe of pardon and forgiuenes
Desyering you to impute it to my simple and rude dulines
I haue forgotten what I haue thought to haue sayed
And am therof full ill a paied   735
But whan I lost my selfe I knew verie well
I lost also that I should you tell

Dame Coye

Why thou wrechid villen doest thou me scorne and moke
To make me to these folke a laufyng stocke

Ere thou go out of my handes ye shalt haue sum thynge   740
And I woll rekine better in the mornynge

�֎ Careawaie

And yf you bete mee maysteris a vise you
For I am none of your seruaunts now
That other I is now your page
And I am no longer in your bondage   745

Dame Coye

Now walke precious thife get thee out of my syght
And I charge thee cum in my presens no more this night
Get thee hens and wayte on thy maister at ons

❡ Careawaie

Mary syr this is handeling for the noons
I wold I had byn hanged before yt I was lost   750
I was neuer this canuased and tost
That if my maister on his part also
Handle me as my maisteris and the other I do
I shall surelye be killed bitwine theim thre
And all the diuels in hell shal not saue me   755
But yet if the other I might haue wt me parte
All this wold neuer greue my harte

✖ Jacke iugler

Hou saye you maisters I pray you tell
Haue not I requited my marchent well
Haue not I handelyd hym after a good sort   760
Had it not byne pytie to haue lost this sporte
A none his maister on his behalphe
You shall see how he woll handle the calphe

yf he throughlye angered bee
He woll make him smart so mot I thee   765
I wold not for the price of a new payre of shone
That any parte of this had bynne vndune
But now I haue reuenged my quarell
I woll go do of this myne apparell
And now let Careawaye be Careawaye againe   770
I haue done with that name now certayne
Except perauenture I shall take the selfe same wede
Sum other tyme agayne for a like cause and nede

Boungrace

Why then darist thou to presume too tell mee
That I know is no wyse possible for to bee   775

❊ Careawaye

Now by my truth master I haue told you no lie
And all these folkes knowith as well as I
I had no sooner knoked at the gate
But straight wayes he had me by the pate
Therfore yf you bet me tyll I fart and shyt againe   780
you shall not cause me for any payne
But I woll affirme as I said before
That when I came nere a nother stode at ye dore

Boungrace

Why ye naughtye villaine darest ye affirme to me
that which was neuer sene nor hereafter shalbe   785
That one man may haue too bodies and two faces
And yt one man at on time may be in too placis
Tell me drankest thou any where by the waye

✿ Careawaie

I shreue me if I drake any more the twise to day
Tyll I met euen now with that other I   790
And with him I supped and dranke truelye
But as for you yf you gaue me drinke and meat
As oftentymes as you do me beat
I were the best fed page in all this Cytie
But as touchyng that, you haue on me no pitye   795
And not onlye I but all that do you sarue
For meat and drynke may rather starue

Boungrace

What you saucye malypert knane
Begine you with your maister to prat and raue
your tonge is lyberall and all out of frame   800
I must niddes counger it and make it tame
wher is yt other Careawai yt thou said was here

Careawaye

Now by my chrystendome syr I wot nere

Boungrace

Why canst thou fynde no man to moke but mee

❧ Careawaye

I moke you not maister soo mot I thee   805
Euerye word was trew that I you tolde

Boungrace

Nay I know toyes and pranke of olde
And now thou art not satisfyed nor content
Without regarde of my biddinges and commaudiment

3—2

To haue plaied by the waie as a leude knaue and negliget 810
When I thee on my message home sent
But also woldest willinglye me delude and moke
And make me to all wyse men a laughyng stoke
shewing me suche thinges as in no wise be maie
To ye intent thy leudnes mai turne to iest and play 815
Therfore if yu speake any such thing to me agaie
I promyse it shalbe vnto thy payne

Careawaye

Loo is not he in myserable case
That sarueth suche a maister in any place
that with force wol compel him yt thing to denie 820
That he knoweth true, and hath sine wt his ye

Boungrace

Was it not troiest thou thine owne shadoo

ℂ Careawaye

My shadoo could neuer haue beten me soo

Boungrace

Why by what reason possible may suche a thyng bee

ℂ Careawaye

Nay I maruael and wonder at it more than ye 825
And at the fyrst it dyd me curstelye meaue
Nor I wold myne owne yes in no wyse belyue
Untyll that other I beate me soo
That he made me beliue it whither i wold or no
And if he had your selfe now within his reache 830
He wold make you say so too or ells beshite your breach

¶ Maister Boungrace

I durst a good mede, and a wager laye
That thou laiest doune and sleppest by the waie
And dremid all this that thou haste me tolde

¶ Careawaie

Naye there you lye master if I might be so bold   835
But we ryse so erlye that yf I hadde
I hadde doone well and a wyse ladde
yet mayster I wolde you vnder stood
That I haue all wayes byn trusty and good
And flye as fast as a bere in a cage   840
When so euer you sende me in your message
in faythe as for this that I haue tolde you
I sawe and felte it as waking as I am nowe
For I had noo soner knocked at the gate
But the other I knaue had mee by the pate   845
And I durst to you one a boke swere
That he had byn watching for mee there
Longe ere I came hyden in sum pryuye place
Euen for the nons too haue me by the face

Maister boungrace

Why then thou speakest not with my wyfe   850

¶ Careawaye

No that I dyd not maister by my lyfe
Untyll that other I was gone
And then my maisteris sent me after a none
To waight on you home in the dyuelles name
I wene the dyuell neuer so beate his dame   855

Maister boungrace

And where became that other Careawaye

❋ Careawaye

By myne honestie syr I cannot saye
But I warrant he is now not far hens
He is here amonge this cumpany for .xl. pens

Maister boungrace

Hence at tonce sike and smell him out   860
I shall rape thee on the lying knanes snought
I woll not bee deludyd with such a glosing lye
Nor giue credens tyll I see it with my oune iye

❋ Careawaie

Trulye good syr by your maistershipps fauoure
I cannot well fynd a knaue by the sauoure   865
Many here smell strong but none so ranke as he
A stronger sented knaue then he was cannot bee
But syr yf he be happelye founde anone
what a meds shal I haue for yt you haue me don

Maister boungrace

If he may befound I shall walke his cote   870

❋ Careawaie

Ye for our ladi sake syr I bisiche you spare hi not
For it is sum false knaue withouten doubt
I had rather the .xl. pens we could find him out
For yf a man maye beliue a glase
Euin my verie oune selfe it was.   875

And here he was but euyn right now
And steped a waye sodenlie I wat not how
Of such a other thīg I haue nether hard ne sene
By our blyssyd lady heauen quene

Maister boungrace

Plainelye it was thy shadow that thou didest se   880
For in faith the other thyng is not possible to be

✻ Careawaye

Yes in good faith syr by your leaue
I know it was I by my apples in my sleue
And speakith as like me as euer you harde
Suche here, such a Cape, such Hose and cote   885
And in eueri thing as iust as .iiii. pens to a grot
That if he were here you should well see
That you could not discern nor know hī frō me
For thinke you that I do not my selfe knowe
I am not so folishe a knaue I trowe   890
Let who woll looke him by and by
And he woll depose vpon a boke that he is I
And I dare well say you woll saye the same
For he called hym selfe by my owne name
And tolde me all that I haue done   895
Sith fyue of the cloke this after none
He could tell when you were to supper sete
you send me home my maisteris to fete
And shewed me al thinges that I dyd by ye waie

Boungrace

What was that

✳ Careawaie

How I dyd at the Bukelers playe   900
And wha I scaterid a basket of apples frō a stal
And gethered them into my sleue all
And how I played after that also

Boungrace

Thou shalt haue by therfore so mote I go
Is that the guise of a trustie page   905
To playe when he is sent on his maisters message

Dame coye

Laye on and spare not for the loue of chryst
Joll his hed to a post, and fauoure your fyste
Now for my sake swete hart spare and fauoure your hand
And lay him about the rybbes with this wande   910

☾ Careawaye

Now marcy that I aske of you both twaine
Saue my lyfe and let me not be slayne
I haue had beting ynough for one daye
That a mischife take the other me Careawayne
That if euer he cume to my handes agayne   915
I wis it shalbe to his payne
But I maruayll greatlye by our lorde Ihesus
How he I escapid, I me beat me thus
And is not he I an vnkind knaue
That woll no more pytie on my selfe haue   920

Here may you see, euidentlye ywis
That in him me no drope of honestie is
Now a vengaûce light on suche a churles knaue
That no more loue toward my selfe haue

Dame coye

I knew verye wel swite hart and saied right now 925
That no fault therof should be in you

Boungrace

No truelye good bedfelow, I were then mutch vnkinde
yf you at any tyme should be out of my mynde

Dame Coye

Surelye I haue of you a great treasure
For you do all thinges which may be to my pleasure 930

Boungrace

I am sory that your chaunce hath now byne so yll
I wolde gladly byne vnsupped, soo you had your fyll
But goo we in pigesnie that you may suppe
you hane cause now to thanke this same hange vppe
For had not he byne you had faryd very well 935

Dame Coye

I bequeth him wt a hot vengaunce to the diuell of hell
And hartelye I besiche him that hanged on the rode
That he neuer eate nor drynke, that may do him good
And that he dye a shamefull dethe sauing my cheryte

⦗ Careawaie

I pray god send him suche prosperitie   940
That hath caused me to haue all this busines
But yet syrs you see the charitye of my maistris
She liueth after a wonderfull charitable facion
For I assure you she is alwayes in this passion
And scacelye on daye throughout the hole yere   945
She woll wyshe any man better chere
And sum tyme yf she well angred bee
I pray god (woll she saye) ye house may sinke vnder mee
But maysters yf you happen to see that other I
As that you shall it is not verye likelye   950
Nor I woll not desyre you for him purposelye to looke
For it is an vncomperable vnhappye hooke
And if it be I, you might happin to seeke
And not fynd me out in an hole weeke
For whan I was wonte to rune a waye   955
I vsed not to cum a gayne in lesse thã a moneth or tway
Houbeit for all this I thinke it be not I
For to shew the matter in dyde trulye
I neuer vse to rune awaye in wynter nor in vere
But all wayes in suche tyme and season of the yere   960
When honye lyeth in the hiues of Bees
And all maner frute falleth from the trees
As Apples, Nuttes, Peres, and plummes also
Wherby a boye maye liue a brod a moneth or two
This cast do I vse I woll not with you fayne   965
Therfore I wonder if he be I sertaine
But and if he be, and you mete me a brod by chaunce

Send me home to my waister with a vengaunce
And shew him if he cume not ere to morowe night
I woll neuer receyue him agayne if I myght 970
And in the meane time I woll giue him a grote
That woll well and thryftelye walke his cote
For a more vngracious knaue is not euen now
Bytwene this place and Calycow
Nor a more frantike mad knaue in bedelem 975
Nor a more folle hence to Iherusalem
That if to cume agayne, parcace he shall refuse
I woll continew as I am and let hym choose
And but he cum the soner by our lady bright
He shall lye without the dores all nyght 980
For I woll shit vp the gate, and get me to bede
For I promisse you I haue a very gydie hede
I nede no supper for this nyght
Nor wolde eate no meat though I myght
And for you also maister I thinke I best 985
you go to bede, and take your rest
For who of you had byn handelid as I haue ben
wold not be long out of his bede I ween
No more woll I but stele out of syght
I praye god geue you all good nyght 990
And send you better hape, and fortune
The to lesse your selfe homeward as I haue don

Sumwhat it was sayeth the prouerbe olde
That the Catte winked when here iye was out
That is to saye no tale can be tolde 995
But that sum Englyshe maye be piked therof out

yfso to serche the laten and ground of it men wil go aboute
As this trifling enterlud yt before you hath bine rehersed
May signifie sum further meaning if it be well serched

Such is the fashyon of the worlde now a dayes   1000
That the symple innosaintes ar deluded
And an hundred thousand diuers wayes
By suttle and craftye meanes shamefullie abused
And by strength force, and violence oft tymes compelled
To beliue aud saye the moune is made of a grene chese 1005
Or ells haue great harme, and parcace their life lese

And an olde saying it is, that most tymes myght
Force, strength, power, and colorable subtlete
Dothe oppresse, debare, ouercum and defeate ryght
Though ye cause stand neuer so greatlye a gainst equite 1010
and ye truth therof be knowẽ for neuer so p̃fit certantye
ye & the pore semple innocent ye hath had wrong & iniuri
Must cal ye other his good maister for shewing hym such
    marcye

And as it is daylie syne for fere of ferther disprofite
He must that man his best frende and maister call   1015
Of whome he neuer receiued any maner benefite
And at whose hand he neuer han any good at all
And must graunt, affirme, or denie, what soeuer he shall
He must saye the Croue is whight, yf he be so cõmanded
ye and that he him selfe is into a nother body chaunged 1020

He must saye he dyd a mysse, though he neuer dyd offend
He must aske forgeuenes, where he did no trespace
Or ells be in troble, care and meserye with out ende

And be cast in sum arrierage, without any grace
And that thing he sawe done before his owne face   1025
He must by compulsion, stifelie denye
And for feare whether he woll or not saye tonge you lye

And in euerye faculte, this thing is put in vre
And is so vniuersall that I nede no one to name
And as I fere is like euermore to endure   1030
For it is in all faculties a commyn sporte and gaine
The weker to saie as ye strōger biddeth, or to haue blam
As a cunning sophist woll by argument bring to passe
That the rude shal confesse, and graunt him selfe an asse

And this is ye daylie excersise and practise of their scoles 1035
And not emongs them onlie, but also emong all others
The stronger to compell and make poore symple foles
To say as they commaund them in all maner matiers
I woll name none particular, but set them all togithers
with out any exception, for I praye you shewe me one 1040
Emonges al in the worlde that vsethe not suche fasion

He that is stronger and more of power and might
Yf he be disposed to reuenge his cause
wollsone pike a quarell be it wronge or right
To the inferior and weker for a cople of straues   1045
And woll agaynst him so extremelie lay the lawes
That he wol put him to the worse, other by false iniurie
Or by some craft and subtelete, or ells by plaine teranie

As you sawe right now, by example playne
An other felowe being a counterfeat page   1050
Brought the gentylmans seruaunt out of his brayne

And made him graunt yt him selfe was fallen in dotage
Baryng him selfe in hand that he dyd rage
And when he could not bryng that to passe by reason
He made him graunt it, and saye by compulsyon   1055

Therfore happy are they that can beware
Into whose handes they fall by any suche chaunce
which if they do, they hardlye escape care
Troble, Miserye, and wofull greuaunce
And thus I make an end, cōmitting you to his gidaū   1060
That made, and redemed vs al, and to you yt be now here
I praye god graunt, and send many a good newe yere.

�֍ Finis

℃ Imprinted at London in Lothbury by me
Wyllyam Copland
* *
*

NOTES

Title. *Jacke Jugeler.* Cf. *Piers the Plowman* A-text, VII. 65, 'Jacke the iogelour'; B-text, VI. 72, 'Jakke the iogeloure'; C-text, IX. 71, 'Jack the iogelour.'

1. *Interpone tuis, &c.* Cf. *Piers the Plowman*, B-text, XII. 21, 'Catoun conforted his sone · that, clerke though he were, To solacen hym sum tyme · as I do whan I make; *Interpone tuis interdum gaudia curis, etc.*' From Dionysii Catonis Disticha de Moribus ad Filium, iii. 7.

7. *percace.* A favourite word with Udall. Occurs five times in this play, l. 7, 62, 375, 977, 1006; nine times in the *Apophthegmes*; eight times in the *Floures for Latine Spekynge*, where it is used to translate *forsan* (3), *fortasse* (3), *forte*, and *at enim* ('marye but percase'). Used twice by Heywood. Variants are 'put case,' 'par case,' 'set case.'

9. *boke of Cato*, the 'so-called *Catonis Disticha*, a school collection of moral maxims, each consisting of two hexameters, in four books.' Teuffel-Schwabe, *Hist. Rom. Lit.* § 398.

10. *emongs.* Cf. l. 13, 258, 1036, 1041.

17. *niddes*, needs. O.E. *nīed.* Cf. l. 24, 141.

25. *industruis*, a misprint for *industrius*, which Grosart reads.

27. *Quod caret, &c.* Ovid, *Heroides*, IV. 89.

28. *Ouyd.* Grosart misreads as *Duyd*, and explains as = David.

32. *verament*, truly. Chaucer, *C. T.*, B. 1903. Greene, *Friar Bacon*, VII. 73. This stanza is defective by a line.

42. *Cicero Tullius.* Cf. Udall, *Apophthegmes*, f. 279, '*Marcus Tullius* in ye thirde booke of that his werke entitleed, *de officiis*, (that is to saie, of honeste behauour, or, how eche manne ought to vse and to demeane hymselfe.'

46. *offirme*, affirm.

50. *commendeth ye old cōmedie.* Cicero, *de Officiis*, I. § 104.

53. *The*, they. Cf. l. 55.

55. *conueiaunce*, artful management. See the soliloquy of Crafty Conueyaunce in Skelton, *Magnyfycence*, 1343—1390. Cf. *Roister Doister*, IV. vi. 16.

61. *not worth an oyster shel.* A common form of expression. We find, 'not worth-ams ase, bean, blewe point, brass pin, button, Childe of Bristowe, cockly fose, crakt nut, cue, cowpyll of onyons, cress, chip, fable, Flanders pin, gnat, grote, grey grote, haddock, halfpeny knyfe, halfpenyworth of ale, his two ears, hen, leke, lekys blade, louse, myteyng, makerell, onion, plukked hen, preine, rottyn wardon, shyttel cocke, sowre calstocke, straw, three halfpence, thre skyppes of a pye, torde, two butterflies, ii kues, two plummis, tail of a fly, whystle, wyteyng.'

64. *Plautus first cōmedie,* i.e. the Amphitruo. The plays of Plautus are arranged in the MSS. in nearly alphabetical order.

65. *scentence.* Cf. *scent, scythe, scite, scituation.*

66. *quesie.* Palsgrave, 'Quaisy as meate or drinke is—*dangereux.*'

69. *merie & glad.* Cf. *Roister Doister,* I. i. 59, 'I can when I will make him mery and glad.' *Tales and Quicke Answeres* (ed. Hazlitt, p. 108), 'He sayde they were merye and gladde.'

76. *besime. Prompt. Parv.* (ed. Way), 'BECEMYN. *Decet.*'

litle boyes. Cf. *The Children of the Chapel Stript and Whipt* (1569), quoted by Steevens on *Hamlet* II. ii. 327, 'Euen in her maiesties chapel do these pretty upstart youthes profane the Lordes day...in feigning bawdie fables gathered from the idolatrous heathen poets.' Machyn's *Diary* (ed. Camden Society, p. 206), Aug. 5th 1559, 'and a play of the chylderyn of Powlles and ther master Se[bastian], master Phelypes, and master Haywod.'

81. *or,* ere. In *Piers the Plowman* the C-text (VIII. 66) has 'or daye,' the B-text (V. 459) 'er day,' the A-text (V. 232) 'ar day.'

84. *sainte Jhone.* From the mention of 'saint Steuen' (l. 86), and the last line of the play, 'I praye god graunt, and send many a good newe yere,' it may be inferred that it was written to be acted on or about the festival of St Stephen (Dec. 26), or St John (Dec. 27).

85. *Rest you merye.* Udall, *Floures for Latine Spekynge,* 'Amice salue. Good felow god you saue, or, o louynge frend god rest you mery.'

90. *crosses of fleshe bone and blod,* i.e. his fingers. Cf. l. 418, 'by thes x. bons'; l. 559, 'by these tene bones.'

107. *iugling cast.* Cf. l. 263. Udall, *Preface to the Translation of the Paraphrase of Erasmus upon Luke,* fol. li (*b*), 'a jugleying cast.' So in fol. clxxviii.

108. *cunger,* i.e. conjure, 'affect by invocation or incantation, charm, bewitch' (*N.E.D.*) 'I beleiue m^r Juggler yo^u haue mette wth one will Coniure yo^u now.' *The Birth of Hercules* (Malone Society), 2170.

moull, i.e. mole. 'These Beasts are all blinde and want eyes, and therefore came the proverb *Talpa caecior, Tuphloteros aspalacos,* blinder then a Mole ;

to signifie a man without all judgement, wit or foresight ; for it is most elegantly applyed to the minde.' Topsell, *History of Four-footed Beasts*, p. 389.

god before. Cf. l. 694. Udall, *Apophthegmes*, f. 152, 'For the grekes saien σὺν θεοῖς, with the Goddes, for that we saye in englyshe, Goddes pleasure beeyng so, or, by the wyll and grace of God, or, and God before, or, God saiyng amen.' Heywood, *The Pardoner and the Friar* (Hazl. Dodsl. I. 236), ' I will never come hither more, While I live, and God before.'

114. *Jenkine,* diminutive of ' John.' Spelt ' Ianekin,' ' Iankin ' in Chaucer.

Carreawaie. Prompt. Parv. ' CARE-AWEY, sorowles. *Tristicia procul.'*

cursed. Cotgrave, ' Mauvais : m. aise : f. *Naughty, bad, lewd, ill ; shrewd, mischievous, hurtful, unhappy, knavish, curst, churlish, cross, froward, stubborn, obstinate, overthwart ; malicious ; depraved, corrupt, mard.'*

116. *vnhappy wage.* Cf. *The Famous History of Doctor Faustus,* Ch. VIII., ' Faustus kept a boy with him, that was his scholar, an unhappy wag, called Christopher Wagner.' In the *Faustbuch* ' ein verwegener Lecker.'

vnhappy. Cf. l. 689, 952, 'vnhappye hooke.' Palsgrave, ' Unhappy of maners—m. *mauluays,* f. *mauluaise s.*' In *Nice Wanton* (Hazl. Dodsl. II. 166), ' unhappy children' are said to be 'unthrifty and disobedient.' *Thersites* (Hazl. Dodsl. I. 412), 'thou unhappy beast' [of the snail]. *Hickscorner* (*ib.* 163), ' unhappy company.' *A Supplycacion &c.* (E. E. T. S. p. 40), ' vnhappy dronckerdes.' Lindesay, *Ane Satyre,* 4226, 4232, ' curst vnhappie wyfe.' Cf. l. 963, 1860. Barclay, *Ship of Fools* (ed. Jamieson, II. 159), ' vnhappy vyce.'

wage. Cotgrave, 'Goinfre : m. *A wag, slipstring, knavish lad.'* 'Sagoin, & Sagouin. *A little Marmoset ; and thence a little crackrope, slipstring, knavish wag, unhappy lad.'*

135. *the Buklers.* 'The youthes of this citie also have used on holy dayes after evening prayer, at their maysters dores, to exercise their wasters and bucklers.' Stowe's *London,* p. 70. [Quoted by Nares, *s.v. Wasters.*] See engraving 89 in Strutt's *Sports and Pastimes* (ed. 1834, p. 262). Cf. *The World and the Child* (Hazl. Dodsl. I. 261), 'And thereto a curious buckler-player I am.' Gifford, *A Posie of Gilloflowers* (Miscellanies of the Fuller Worthies' Library, ed. Grosart, I. 148), ' To tosse the buckler and the blade.' *Tell-trothes New-yeares Gift* (New Shakespeare Society, p. 30), 'Others builde their knauery on other mens misfortune, that are matched with Ioone, *communis omnibus,* that could play at bucklers so soone as she was past her cradell.'

137. *my cosune.* Cf. *Roister Doister,* III. i. 4, 'my cousin Roister Doister.' Of course Jacke Jugeler is no more cousin of Jenkine Careawaie than Mathewe Merygreeke is of Roister Doister.

W. J. J.   4

145. *faire toche.* Cf. *The World and the Child* (Hazl. Dodsl. I. 262), 'How sayest thou now, Folly, hast thou not a touch ?' [i.e. at buckler-play]. Udall, *Apophthegmes*, f. 105, 'yea and for a faire touche, by deceiuyng & beguylyng their prince.'

147. *had wrong.* Palsgrave, 'I haue wronge, a person doth me wronge or iniurye. *On me fait tort.*' Cf. Heywood, *Epigrammes vpon Prouerbes* (ed. Spenser Society, p. 135), 'Thou art at an ebbe in Newgate, thou hast wrong.'

148. *cokes prceious potstike.* Cf. *Roister Doister*, III. iv. 127, 'By cocks precious potsticke.' Palsgrave, 'Potstycke—*batton* s., m.' 'The precious potstick is probably the rod on which the sponge was lifted up, a common symbol of the Passion.' (*Skeat*.) Cf. 593. 'prceious' is of course a misprint for 'precious.' Grosart explains *potstike* as 'potsick'=tipsy.

152. *Freuteres.* Palsgrave, 'Frutrer that selleth frute—*fruyctier* s., m.'

159. *faryng.* Palsgrave, 'I fare, I playe at a game so named, "at the dyse." *Ie joue aux dez.*' Grosart says='fairing or gift-purchases, as at a Fair.'

at all. Cf. *The Nice Wanton* (Hazl. Dodsl. II. 171), 'eleven at all.' Skelton, *Bowge of Courte*, 348, 'Now haue at all.' Cf. 391.

163. *swere and stare.* A common phrase. Cf. Skelton, *Bowge of Courte*, 381, 'Thou muste swere and stare, man, al daye longe.' *Magnyfycence*, 419, 'counterfet lye, Swere and stare, and byde therby.' *Why Come Ye &c.*, 100, 'With sweryngne and starynge.' *Like Will to Like* (Hazl. Dodsl. III. 324). *Terence in English* (Phormio v. viii.), 'swearing and staring like caualleers. *Hi gladiatorio animo ad me adfectant uiam.*' Nashe, *Pierce Penilesse* (ed. McKerrow, I. 170), 'sweares and stares after ten in the hundreth.'

169. *euery dell.* Cf. l. 305. Palsgrave, 'Every deale, *tout tant quil y a.*'

171. *Sartayde,* misprint for 'sartayne'=certain.

behynde, unpaid. Palsgrave, 'I am behynde, as money that remayneth onpayed of a somme.' Skelton, *Magnyfycence*, 2322, 'behynde of thy rente.'

174. *This*=these. Cf. l. 194. *Piers the Plowman*, Prol. A-text, 59, B-text 62, C-text 60, 'this maistres.'

177. *For the nons,* purposely, intentionally. *Prompt. Parv.* 'FOR THE NONYS. *Idcirco, ex proposito.*' Horman, *Vulg.* 'for the nonis, *dedita opera.*' Also, '*de industria.*' M.E. *for pan anes.*

181. *starke staryng mad.* Cf. Heywood, *Epigrammes* (Spenser Society, p. 113), 'starke staryng blinde.' Skelton, *Agaynst the Scottes*, 143, 'starke mad.' Barclay, *Ship of Fools* (ed. Jamieson, I. 96), 'starynge mad.'

183. *whether*=whither.

191. *my simithe*=meseemeth. (Grosart says=simathin=partiality or liking.)

198. *forthest.* Cf. Chaucer, *Boethius* (ed. Skeat), IV. pr. vi. 86, 91.

200. *hei hei.* Cf. *The Trial of Treasure* (Hazl. Dodsl. III. 273), 'Hey, lusty lad, how fresh am I now !' *Shirburn Ballads* (ed. Clark), p. 271, 'His talke is never sorrowfull, But Heigh ! at every word.'

205. *were,* O.E. wǣre.

206. *abye.* Palsgrave, 'I ABYE, I forthynke or am punished for a thynge.' Cf. *Roister Doister*, II. iv. 21, 'full truly abye thou shalt.'

207. *sumpretie,* read *sum pretie.*

211. *lyne,* cease. Cf. Udall, *Apophthegmes,* f. 77, 'He neuer lynned rehatyng.' *Ib.* f. 226, 'would in no wyse lynne pratyng therof.' *The Rare Triumphs of Love and Fortune* (Hazl. Dodsl. VI. 234), 'I would never lin.' O.E. *linnan.*

217. *gingerlie.* Cf. *The Interlude of Youth,* 411, 'iwis ye go ful gingerlie' (with Bang's note). Skelton, *Garlande of Laurell,* 1203, 'With, Gingirly, go gingerly !...go she neuer so gingirly.' *The Four Elements* (Hazl. Dodsl. I. 47), 'I can dance it gingerly.' Udall, *Floures for Latine Spekynge, 'Tenero ac molli passu suspendimus gradum.* We staye and prolonge our goinge with a nyce or tendre and softe, delicate, or gingerly pace.' Nashe, *Pierce Penilesse* (ed. McKerrow, I. 173), 'Mistris Minx...that lookes as simperingly as if she were besmeard, and iets it as gingerly as if she were dancing the Canaries.'

saint Loye. Cf. Chaucer, *C. T.,* Prol. 120, 'Hir gretteste ooth was but by seynt Loy' (with Skeat's note). *The Conflict of Conscience* (Hazl. Dodsl. VI. 75), 'Sent Loy save your horse.' Bale, *Kynge Johan* (ed. Camden Society), p. 75. *Early English Popular Poetry* (ed. Hazlitt), III. 236. Nashe, *Lenten Stuffe* (ed. McKerrow, p. 148).

218. *halpeny worth of siluer spoons.* Heywood, *Proverbs* (Spenser Society, p. 81), 'Yet was she nowe, sodeinly waxen as nyse As it had bene a halporth of syluer spoones.'

219. *vengable.* As adverb in Udall, *Apophthegmes,* f. 7 ; Heywood, *Epigrammes* (ed. Spenser Society, pp. 103, 155, 180). As adjective in l. 321 ; *Gammer Gurton's Needle,* III. ii. 10 ; *Trial of Treasure* (Hazl. Dodsl. III. 273) ; *Locrine,* I. ii. (ed. Tauchnitz, p. 140) ; Udall, *Apophthegmes,* f. 49.

224. *Aulsoon,* spelt 'Ales' on the title-page, 'Alis,' l. 658. Cf. Chaucer, *C. T.,* D, 530, 548.

tripe and goo. Cf. *Two angrie Women of Abington* (Malone Society), 1979, 'Nay then trip and go.'

226. *simperith.* Cotgrave, 'Faire la petite bouche. *To mince or simper it.*'

prankith. Cf. *The Four Elements* (Hazl. Dodsl. I. 47), 'I can prank it properly.' *Appius and Virginia* (*ib.* IV. 124), 'farewell, go prank ye.' Nashe, *Pierce Penilesse* (ed. McKerrow, p. 173), 'spends halfe a day in pranking her selfe.'

getteth, jetteth. This is the M.E. spelling. *Prompt. Parv.* 'GETTYN. *Verno, lassivo, gesticulo.*' See also IETTYN, with Way's note. Palsgrave, 'I get, I use a proude countenaunce and pace in my goyng. *Je braggue.*' Heywood, *Play of the Weather* (Early English Dramatists, p. 121), 'Then would we jet the streets trim as a parrot.' *Roister Doister,* III. iii. 121, 'Then must ye stately goe, ietting vp and downe.'

228. *minceth.* Cotgrave, 'Aller à pas menu. *To tread gingerly, to mince it like a maid.*' *The Disobedient Child* (Hazl. Dodsl. II. 290), 'this mincing trull.' Preface to Bernard's *Terence in English,* 'the minsing mynion.' Isaiah iii. 16 (Authorised Version), 'mincing as they go.'

brideleth. Cf. Skelton, *Against Garnesche* (ed. Dyce, I. 122), 'Sche seyd how ye ded brydell, moche lyke a dromadary.' Nashe, *Have with you to Saffron Walden* (ed. McKerrow, III. 70), 'some little coy bridling of the chin and nice simpring.' Cotgrave, 'Se rengorger. *To hold down the head, or thrust the chin into the neck, as some do in pride, or to make their faces look the fuller; we say, to bridle it.*'

swimmeth. Cf. *Roister Doister,* II. iii. 46, 'ye shall see hir glide and swimme.' Gascoigne, *Supposes* (ed. Hazlitt, I. 206), 'They swimme in silke, when others royst in ragges.' Overbury, *Characters* (ed. Rimbault, p. 50), 'Her lightnesse gets her to swim at top of the table.' *Two Noble Kinsmen,* III. v. 28, 'Swim with your bodies.' Massinger, *The Bondman,* III. iii., 'Carry your bodies swimming.' Shirley, *The Ball,* II. iii., 'Carry your body in the swimming fashion.'

229. *tredith...a wrye.* Cotgrave, 'Mesmarcher. *To tread, or go awry, to set the steps amiss.*'

here, hair. M.E. *heer, her.*

tryppeth like a do. Cf. Peile, *David and Bethsabe,* I. i. 92, 'Now comes my lover tripping like the roe.'

231. *wardelith,* a misprint for 'warbelith Cotgrave, 'Gringoter. *To warble, quaver, shake with the voice.*'

galiard, 'a quick and lively dance in triple time.' (*N.E.D.*) *Twelfth Night,* I. iii. 112; *Much Ado,* II. i. 69. *Orchestra* (Arber, *English Garner,* V. 40, §§ 67, 68), 'Oft does she make her body upward flyne With lofty turns and caprioles in the air.'

234. *chatteth like a Pye.* Cf. Skelton, *Phyllyp Sparowe,* 397, 'The fleckyd pye to chatter.'

235. *parat Poppagaye.* Cf. Skelton, *Speke Parrot,* 108, 'Parrot, Parrot,

Parrot, praty popigay'! *Ib.* 172, 'Parrot the popagaye.' Cotgrave, 'Papegay : m. *A Parrot, or Popingay.*'

236. Cf. *Roister Doister*, III. iv. 4, 'Hir talke is as fine as she had learned in schooles.'

237. *fle,* fly. M.E. *fleen.*

239. *tael,* misprint for 'tale.'

by, against.

244. *Therfore I woll here &c.* Plautus, Amphitruo, 201, '*sed quo modo et uerbis quibus me deceat fabularier, | prius ipse mecum etiam uolo hic meditari.*'

249. *I may giue my life, &c.* Udall, *Floures for Latine Spekynge,* 'ego perierim, I am vtterlye vndone, or I may gyue my lyfe for an halfepeny.' *Apophthegmes,* f. 162, 'farewell his life for an halfpenie.'

257. *tow,* misprint for 'two.'

258. *my thought,* methought. Cf. l. 191.

bysye, i.e. [he was] busy. Hazlitt unnecessarily changes to 'I see.'

262. *grudgid.* Palsgrave, 'I GRUTCHE, I repyne agaynst a thyng.' Skelton, *Why Come Ye,* 249, 'They grugyd, and sayde Theyr wages were nat payde.'

263. *light cast playe.* Cf. l. 107.

267. *setteth nothing by.* Palsgrave, 'I set by, or have in estymacyon. *Jaconte,* or, *jaccompte.*'

269. *rufflers. Manipulus Vocabulorum,* 'A RUFFLER, *elatus, a, lasciuus.*'

275. *bouncing.* 'Often also (like "thumping, whacking, whopping, strapping," and other words meaning vigorous striking), used with the sense of "big," esp. "big rather than elegant or graceful."' *N.E.D.*

277. *god yld it you.* Palsgrave, 'But, for God yelde you, whiche we use by maner of thankyng of a person, they use *Grant mercy,* or *grans mercys,* understandynge *je vous rens grans mercys.*' *Macbeth,* I. vi. 13. 'How you shall bid God-eyld vs for your paines.'

285. *costerds. Prompt. Parv.* 'COSTARD, appulle.' *Cath. Angl.* 'COSTERD; quererarium.'

293. *syr,* used in addressing a woman, as 'brother' in *Roister Doister,* I. ii. 120. Cf. 'sirs' in *Love's Labour's Lost,* IV. iii. 211 ; *Antony and Cleopatra,* IV. xv. 85.

arayed. 'Array. To put into a (sore) plight, trouble, afflict.' *N.E.D.,* which quotes Udall, *Erasm. Par.,* Luke xiii. 11, 'Araied with a disease both incurable and peiteous to see.' Add *Apophthegmes,* f. 315, 'eiuill araied with Cicero his iestyng.'

304. *face it.* Palsgrave, 'I face one with a lye, I make hym byleve a lye is trewe.'

308. *muse.* Cotgrave, 'Muser. *To muse, dream, study, bethink himself of; to pawse, or linger about a matter.*'

310. *stoding,* studying. *Prompt. Parv.* 'STODYYN̄'. *Studeo.*' *Piers the Plowman,* A-text, XII. 6, 'loth for to stodie.' Hazlitt reads 'stewing' without comment.

314. *giue...a flye.* Cf. *Thersites* (Hazl. Dodsl. I. 400), 'set not by them a fly.' *Nice Wanton* (*ib.* II. 167), 'By your malice they shall not set a fly.'

317. *saint George ye boroue,* i.e. 'St George [be] the surety.' The usual expression is 'Saint George to borow.' Cf. *Roister Doister,* IV. viii. 45, 'sainct George to borow, our Ladies knight.' Skelton, *Howe the Douty Duke of Albany, &c.* 506 (ed. Dyce, II. 83), 'And thus, Sainct George to borowe.'

318. *ieopard.* Palsgrave, 'I Jeparde, I adventure.' *Roister Doister,* IV. viii. 17, 'I durst ieoparde my hande.' *Jacob and Esau* (Hazl. Dodsl. II. 252), 'I dare jeopard a groat.' Cf. l. 358.

bee as bee maye. Heywood, *Epigrammes* (Spenser Society, p. 166), 'Be as be may is no bannynge.'

323. *swete mete, &c.* Heywood, *Proverbs* (Spenser Society, p. 16), 'Sweete meate will haue sowre sawce.' *Ib. Epigrammes,* pp. 158—9. Skelton, *Colyn Cloute,* 450, 'Yet swete meate hath soure sauce.' Harman, *Caveat for Cursetors* (ed. Hindley, p. 95), 'according to the proverb, that sweet meat will have sour sauce.' Bernard, *Terence in English,* p. 93, '*Aegritudo gaudio intercesserit.* Sorrow is mixt with ioy. Sweet meat hath a sowre sauce.' Camden, *Remaines* (ed. 1637, p. 305), 'sweet meate will have sowre sauce.'

325. *cape,* cap. 'The words *cap, cape, cope* were all the same originally.' (Skeat.)

331. *soft,* from the imperatival use of the adverb='hold, stop,' came to be used as a verb. Grosart misreads as 'holt.'

334. *chafed.* Palsgrave, 'I CHAFE with the heate of fyre, or I provoke and move to anger. *Jeschauffe.*' Grosart says, 'it may be *chased,*' which is not the case.

341. *lookes,* misprint for 'lockes.' 'Lokkes' is used as equivalent to 'head' in *Piers the Plowman,* A-text, II. 84, 'serwe on thi lokkes.'

by the swet lookes. Cf. Heywood, *The Pardoner and the Friar* (Hazl. Dodsl. I. 231), 'Ish lug thee by the sweet ears.' Gosson, *Schoole of Abuse* (ed. Arber, p. 33), 'placed Apelles the player by his own sweete sides.' *Ib.* p. 54, 'we lay holde on his locks, turn him away with his backe full of stripes.'

345. *set by hym.* Palsgrave, 'I set by one, I estyme hym, or regarde hym. *Je tiens compte.*' Cf. *Thersites,* quoted on l. 314.

347. *See how he beginnith, &c.* Amph. 308, '*cingitur: certe expedit se.*'

348. *makith buttens.* Amph. 295, '*timet homo.*' Cf. *Like will to Like* (Hazl. Dodsl. III. 317), 'My buttock made buttons of the new fashion.' *Grim, the Collier of Croydon* (Hazl. Dodsl. VIII. 435), 'Alas, my breech makes buttons.' Ray, *English Proverbs* (ed. 1768), p. 179.

349. *out at his heele.* *Roister Doister*, III. iii. 96, 'I might feele Your soule departing within an inche of your heele.'

353. *A more dastard, &c.* Amph. 293, '*nullust hoc metuculosus aeque.*'

355. Ray, *English Proverbs* (ed. 1768), p. 117.

362. *hardelye.* Cf. *Roister Doister*, I. ii. 44, 'Let them hardly take thought.' *Et passim.*

364. *Now fistes, &c.* Amph. 302, '*agite pugni : iam diust quom uentri uictum non datis. | iam pridem uidetur factum, heri quod homines quattuor | in soporem collocastis nudos.*'

369. *for wood*, madly, furiously. *Prompt. Parv.* 'WOODE, or madde. *Amens, furiosus, insanus.*' Cf. Chaucer, *Hous of Fame*, 1747, 'wimmen loven us for wood.' *Legend of Good Women*, 2420.

370. *Four hath he slayne, &c.* Amph. 304, '*formido male, | ne ego hic nomen meum commutem et Quintus fiam e Sosia. | quattuor uiros sopori se dedisse hic autumat : | metuo, ne numerum augeam illum.*'

373. *yers .ii.* The rime shows that this should be read as 'twain.'

378. *fist mete.* Amph. 309, '*quisquis homo huc profecto uenerit, pugnos edet.*' Cf. *Thersites* (Hazl. Dodsl. I. 405), 'knocked bread.'

379. *I haue supped, &c.* Amph. 310, '*apage, non placet me hoc noctis esse : cenaui modo : | proin tu istam cenam largire, si sapis, esurientibus.*'

381. *Yet.* Hazlitt reads 'It,' which is possible (=yt). Is 'it' absorbed in the *t* of 'yet'?

383. *weighith of the best.* Amph. 312, '*haud malum huic est pondus pugno.*'

384. *waghith*, misprint for 'weghith'=weigheth. Amph. 312, '*perii, pugnos ponderat.*' M.E. *weghen.* Hazlitt prints 'waggeth' without comment, and Grosart, who prints 'waghith,' glosses it as 'waggeth.'

385. *with a stroke, &c.* Amph. 318, '*exossatum os esse oportet, quem probe percusseris.*'

our ladye boons. The rime shows that the right reading is 'bandes' =bonds. 'Our Lady's bonds'=parturition, travail. *N.E.D.* quotes '*Will of W. Pryor* (1504), App., I Alys beyng in the bondis of owr lady. Bp. WHITE in Strype, *Eccl. Mem.* III. ii. lxxxi. 286. To dye in the bond, as they call it, of our Lady, and travail of child.' 'Ladye' is of course the M.E. form for 'lady's,' representing the O.E. weak genitive hlæfdigan. Cf. Chaucer, *C.T.*, Prol. 88, 'in his lady grace.'

The corruption of 'bandes' into 'boons' is curious, and seems to suggest that the transcriber or the printer, not understanding the expression ' our ladye bandes,' turned for guidance (which some of our modern editors might have done with advantage) to the original, and finding there *exossatum os*, regardless of rime or sense turned ' bandes' into ' bones.' He may have been influenced by the fact that final *n* often takes a parasitic *d* after it.

387. *Ere ye assaye thē, &c.*   Amph. 324, '*si in me exercituru's, quaeso in parietem ut primum domes.*'

388. *in earnest, or in game.*   Cf. *Tales and Quicke Answeres* (ed. Hazlitt, p. 27), ' between earnest and game.'

395. *a cople of straus.*   Cf. l. 1045, ' for a cople of straues.'

398. *May a man demaund, &c.*   Amph. 346, '*possum scire, quo profectus quoius sis aut quid ueneris ?*'

399. *My maisters seruaunt, &c.*   Amph. 347, ' *huc eo, eri sum seruos.*'

400. *what busynes, &c.*   Amph. 350, '*quid apud hasce aedis negoti est tibi ?*'

401. *Nay mary, &c.*   Amph. 350, '*immo quid tibist ?*'

402. *For I am commaunded, &c.*   Amph. 351, '*ME. rex Creo uigiles nocturnos singulos semper locat.* | *SO. bene facit: quia nos eramus peregri, tutatust domi.*'

405. *well now I am cume, &c.*   Amph. 353, ' *at nunc abi sane, aduenisse familiares dicito.*'

407. *Sewing,* shewing.   The *h* has fallen out.

409. *I cannot tell, &c.*   Amph. 354, ' *nescio quam tu familiaris sis: nisi actutum hinc abis,* | *familiaris accipiere faxo haud familiariter.*'

410. *nere,* nearer.   O.E. *nēar,* comparative of *nēah.*   Sh. *R. II,* III. ii. 64 ; v. i. 8 ; *Mcb.* II. iii. 146.

412. *planly,* plainly.   The *i* has dropped out.

413. *That I am a seruaunt, &c.*   Amph. 356, ' *hic inquam habito ego atque horunc seruos sum.*'

414. *soo god me snache.*   Cf. *Jacob and Esau* (Hazl. Dodsl. II. 253), ' Ye shall run apace then, I ween, so God me snatch.'

but thou goo thee waies, &c.   Amph. 357, ' *faciam ego hodie te superbum, nisi hinc abis.   SO. quonam modo ?* | *ME. auferere, non abibis, si ego fustem sumpsero.*'

418. *l am a seruaunt, &c.*   Amph. 359, ' *quin me esse huius familiai familiarem praedico.*'

by thes .x. bons, i.e. the fingers, more frequently called ' the ten command-ments.'   Cf. l. 559.   Heywood, *The Four P. P.* (Hazl. Dodsl. I. 381), ' Yet, by these ten bones, I could right well, &c.'   *Thersites* (*ib.* 429), ' By this ten bones, She served me once &c.'   Sh. *2 Hen. VI,* I. iii. 193; *Digby Mysteries* (ed. Furnivall), p. 4.

419. *Noo more prating, &c.* Amph. 360, '*uide sis quam mox uapulare uis, nisi actutum hinc abis.*'

at towns, taken by Hazlitt and Grosart as = 'at once' (*attones*), and this is probable, as the Latin has *actutum*, and the word rimes with *bons*.

421. *Pike.* Udall, *Apophthegmes*, f. 127, 'ὦ ξένε τυράννοις ἐκποδὼν καθίστασο. Stand utter ye geast unbidden, picke you hens, Abacke, out of our sight & regall presence.' *Roister Doister*, IV. iii. 90, 'Auaunt lozell, picke thee hence.' *Damon and Pythias* (Hazl. Dodsl. IV. 34), 'pick, rise, and walk.' Palsgrave, 'I PYCKE me forth out of a place, or I pycke me hence. *Je me tyre auant, je me suis tyré auant, tyrer auant.*'

walke. *Tales and Quicke Answeres* (ed. Hazlitt, p. 64), 'walke knaue with a myschiefe.' Skelton, *Howe the Douty Duke of Albany, &c.*, 154, 'Walke, Scot.' Heywood, *Epigrammes* (ed. Spenser Society, p. 106), 'walke foole.' *Wealth and Health* (ed. Malone Society), 415, 'ye shall walke a fleming knaue.'

422. *What wilt thou let me, &c.* Amph. 361, '*tun domo prohibere peregre me aduenientem postulas ?*'

my nowne. *Roister Doister*, I. iii. 32, 'my nowne Annot.' The *n* of the possessive is improperly prefixed to the following word.

423. *bere me a souse.* *Gammer Gurton's Needle*, IV. ii. 74, 'She bare me two or three souses behind in the nape of the necke.'

430. *In nomine patris.* Cf. l. 554. *Roister Doister*, I. iv. 49, 'A pecke ? *Nomine patris*, have ye so much spare ?' Heywood, *Proverbs* (ed. Spenser Society, p. 91).

432. *on a boke swer.* *Tales and Quicke Answeres*, XVII. (ed. Hazlitt, p. 27), 'thou shall swere so vpon this boke ; and held to her a boke....So she toke the boke in her hande and sayd : By this boke, &c.' *Gammer Gurton's Needle*, II. i. 67 ; Nashe, *Pierce Penilesse* (ed. McKerrow, I. p. 165). Cf. l. 449, 892.

434. *Who is thy mayster, &c.* Amph. 362, '*quis erus est igitur tibi ?*'

435. *And thine owne name, &c.* Amph. 364, '*quid nomen tibist ?*'

441. *rage*, sport. *Sir Beues of Hamtoun* (E.E.T.S. p. 4), 'He lovith not with me to rage.' Chaucer, *C. T.*, A, 257, 'And rage he coude, as it were right a whelpe.' *Ib.* 3273, 'rage and pleye'; *ib.* 3958, 'rage or ones pleye.' Skelton, *Why Come Ye*, 33, 'age cannat rage.' *The Four P. P.* (Hazl. Dodsl. I. 343), 'Nay, fore God, then did I rage.'

442. *Take that.* Amph. 370, '*nunc profecto uapula ob mendacium.*'

444. *Darest thou, &c.* Amph. 373, '*tun te audes Sosiam esse dicere, | qui ego sum ?*'

445. *I wolde, &c.* Amph. 380, '*ita di faciant, ut tu potius sis atque ego te ut uerberem.*'

446.　*bet*, beat.　The M.E. form.

452.　*who is thy maister now ?*　Amph. 375, 'quoius nunc es ?'

454.　*I am your owne, &c.*　Amph. 375, 'tuos : nam pugnis usu fecisti tuom.'

457.　*Helpe saue my life, &c.*　Amph. 376, 'pro fidem, Thebani ciues.'

458.　*Why thou lowsy thefe, &c.*　Amph. 376, 'etiam clamas, carnufex ?'

461.　*Ye doest thou make, &c.*　Amph. 381, 'etiam muttis ?'

romeringe, muttering (=*muttis*), for 'romelinge.'　*Prompt. Parv.* 'ROME-LYNGE, or privy mysterynge (preuy mustringe, P.) *Ruminacio, mussitacio,* CATH.'

463.　*In faith now, &c.*　Amph. 381, 'iam tacebo.'　There is no suggestion in the original of the humour of promising to cease and immediately crying, 'helpe, helpe !'

466.　*to see*, probably a misprint for 'to thee.'

468.　*Who art thou now ?*　Amph. 382, 'quid igitur ? qui nunc uocare ?'

469.　*Noo bodye, &c.*　Amph. 382, 'nemo nisi quem iusseris.'

470.　*Thou saydest, &c.*　Amph. 383, 'Amphitruonis te esse aiebas Sosiam.'

471.　*I crye you marcy.*　A common expression of apology for a mistake. Lyly, *Mother Bombie*, IV. ii. 28, 'I crie you mercy, I tooke you for a ioynd stoole.'　Shakespeare, *Lear*, III. vi. 50.

472.　*I said a mysse.*　Amph. 383, 'peccaueram.'

473.　*alwaies.*　The rime shows that this should be 'alwaie.'

479.　*nod*, noddy.　Minsheu, 'a NODDIE, *because he nods when hee should speake.* Vi. FOOLE, DIZARD.'

480.　*I am he, &c.*　Amph. 387, 'ego sum Sosia ille, quem tu dudum esse aiebas mihi.'

482.　*no poynt*, not at all.　Cotgrave, 'Point.　(*An Adverb*) *not, no one jot, by no means, in no manner, not at all.*'　Udall, *Apophthegmes*, f. 137, 'estemed the fruite to bee no poyncte the more polluted.'　*The Rare Triumphs of Love and Fortune* (Hazl. Dodsl. VI. 203), 'Ah, no point good !'　Hazlitt, not understanding the phrase, puts a comma after 'poynt.'

thi witts do thee faylle.　Amph. 386, 'fugit te ratio.'

484.　*But syr myght I be bolde, &c.*　Amph. 388, 'obsecro ut per pacem liceat te alloqui, ut ne uapulem.'

486.　*Truce for a whyle, &c.*　Amph. 389, 'immo indutiae parumper fiant, siquid uis loqui.'　Cf. *Roister Doister*, IV. viii. 33, 'truce for a pissing while or twaine.'

thy for *the* (=thee).　So *nyde* (194), *my* (191, 258), *myruayllus* (259), *commaundyd* (260), *dyd* (293).

487.　*May a man, &c.*　Amph. 391, 'tuae fidei credo ?'

490. *What and you kepe*, &c. Amph 392, '*quid, si falles ?*'

then vpŏ cae, &c. Amph. 392, '*tum Mercurius Sosiae iratus siet.*'

cae. the last letter looks like a broken *r* or *e*. Grosart pronounces it 'unintelligible,' but the rime might have suggested the explanation.

492. *Now dare I speake*, &c. Amph. 393, '*nunc licet mihi libere quiduis loqui. | Amphitruonis ego sum seruos Sosia.*' A colon or full stop should be read after 'speake.'

so mote I thee, so may I thrive. *Prompt. Parv.* 'THEEN̄, or thryvyn̄'. *Vigeo.*' Cf. l. 765, 805. *The World and the Child* (Hazl. Dodsl. I. 264); *The Four P. P.* (*ib.* I. 355); *Interlude of Youth* (*ib.* II. 23, 35); Heywood, *Epigrammes* (ed. Spenser Society, p. 109) ; *A Mery Play* (ed. Whittingham, p. 31) ; Bale, *Kynge Johan* (Camden Society, p. 45).

494. *What saiest thou soo.* Amph. 394, '*etiam denuo ?*'

495. *And yf thou wilt*, &c. Amph. 396, '*ut lubet, quid tibi lubet fac.*'

496. *beate on mee, tyll I stinke.* Cf. *Roister Doister*, IV. iii. 120, 'I shall cloute thee tyll thou stinke.' Heywood, *A Mery Play* (ed. Whittingham, p. 3), 'Bete her, quotha ? yea, that she shall stynke.' *Ib.* p. 4, 'she wyll stynke without any betyng.' *The World and the Child* (Hazl. Dodsl. I. 264), 'I should so beat him with my staff, That all his stones should stink.'

497. *And yet woll I*, &c. Amph. 399, '*certe edepol tu me alienabis numquam quin noster siem.*'

498. *This bedlem knaue*, &c. Amph. 402, '*hic homo sanus non est.*' Cf. Skelton, *Why Come Ye*, 652, 'Suche a madde bedleme.'

514. *Doo not I speake now.* Amph. 407, '*non loquor ?*'

is not this my hande. Amph. 406, '*non mist lanterna in manu ?*'

516. *Did not this other knaue*, &c. Amph. 407, '*nonne hic homo modo me pugnis contudit ?*'

520. *I woll home*, &c. Amph. 409, '*cur non intro eo in nostram domum ?*'

524. *I thou hast.* Hazlitt unnecessarily omits the 'I.' 'I-thou' is a compound to express the dual personality, like 'he-I,' ll. 918—19 ; 'him-me,' l. 922. Cf. l. 550.

538. *He lyeth not a worde*, &c. Amph. 423, '*argumentis uicit.*'

540. *betwene erneste and game.* Cf. *Tales and Quicke Answeres* (ed. Hazlitt, p. 27), 'A certeyne man, whiche vpon a tyme in company betwene ernest and game was called cuckolde.'

541. *I must go sike me*, &c. Amph. 423, '*aliud nomen quaerundumst mihi.*'

550. *I thou.* Hazlitt unnecessarily changes 'I' to 'Ay.' See note on l. 524.

551. *porse.* Spelt 'pors' in *Piers the Plowman*, A-text, v. 110 ; C-text, VII. 199.

552. *Godes bodye.* Cf. Barclay, *Ship of Fools* (ed. Jamieson, p. 96), 'Some swereth armys nayles herte and body, Terynge our lord worse than the Jowes hym arayed.'

556. *How now art thou, &c.* Amph. 433, '*quid nunc? uincon argumentis, te non esse Sosiam ?* '

557. *sayest thou nay to that.* Amph. 434, '*tu negas med esse ?* '

558. *Ye mary, &c.* Amph. 434, '*quid ego ni negem, qui egomet siem ?* '

559. *by these tene bones, &c.* Amph. 435, '*per Iouem iuro med esse.*'

560. *Or ells tell me, &c.* Amph. 438, '*quis ego sum saltem, si non sum Sosia ? te interrogo.*'

562. *By my fayth the same, &c.* Amph. 439, '*ubi ego Sosia nolim esse, tu esto sane Sosia.*'

572. *I haue sene my selfe, &c.* Amph. 442, '*saepe in speculum inspexi : nimis similest mei.*'

574. *He hath in euerye poynt, &c.* Amph. 443, '*itidem habet petasum ac uestitum : tam consimilest atque ego. | sura, pes, statura, tonsus, oculi, nasum, uel labra, | malae, mentum, barba, collus : totus.*'

575. *notted,* closely cut, cropped. Palsgrave, ' I NOTTE ones heed, I clyppe it. *Je tons.*' Cooper, *Thesaurus* (1578), 'Tondere. *To notte his heare shorte.*' See Skeat's note on 'not-heed,' Chaucer, *C. T.*, Prol. 109. Hazlitt, without comment, changes to 'knotted.'

580. *That if he haue, &c.* Amph. 446, '*si tergum cicatricosum, nil hoc similist similius.*'

582. *And yet when I remembre, &c.* Amph. 447, '*sed quom cogito, equidem certo idem sum qui semper fui. | noui erum, noui aedis nostras : sane sapio et sentio. | non ego illi optempero quod loquitur : pultabo foris.*'

584. *fiue witts,* i.e. the five senses, hearing, sight, speech, smelling, feeling, according to Grosseteste, *Castle of Love.* 'But for *speech* we commonly have tasting.' Skeat, *Piers the Plowman*, B-text, I. 15. Cf. XIV. 53, 'of syȝte and of tonge, In etynge and in handlynge · and in alle thi fyue wittis.'

586. *mooke,* misprint for 'mocke.'

590. *precious,* 'often used ironically, implying worthlessness.' (Halliwell.)

slinking. Cotgrave, 'Regnarder. *To play the Fox ; to steal, slip, or slink, aside, upon a guilty conscience, or fear to be taken in the manner.*' Grosart and Hazlitt read 'stinking' without comment. The alliteration supports the reading 'slinking.'

592. *wine shakin,* i.e. 'wind-shaken.' *D* is often lost after *n.* Cf. Skelton, *Against Garnesche* (ed. Dyce, I. 117), 'Your wynde schakyn

shankkes.' Harman, *Caveat* (ed. Hindley, p. 84), 'This ill-favoured wind-shaken knave.' So 'rain-beaten,' in Skelton, *Magnyfycence*, 2218, 'rayne beten iauell'; *Why Come Ye*, 602, ' Ye raynbetyn beggers.'

pecpours, pick-pocket. Palsgrave, 'I PYCKE a purse. *Je fouille en vne bource.*' *Nice Wanton* (Hazl. Dodsl. II. 169), 'I must have some of the money Thou hast picked out of thy father's purse.' Hazlitt erroneously reads the original as ' peepours,' and explains 'pillory-peeper.'

593. *gods precious*, a common oath, some word like 'blood,' 'bones,' 'body,' or 'passion,' (cf. l. 629) being understood. Cf. *Roister Doister*, IV. viii. 40, 'by cocks precious.' *The Disobedient Child* (Hazl. Dodsl. II. 304), 'By God's precious.' Chapman, *Monsieur D'Olive*, v. i. (ed. Pearson, I. 246), 'Gods precious.'

I shall breake thy necke. Amph. 454, '*lumbifragium hinc auferes.*'

602. *Good lorde of heuine, &c.* Amph. 455, '*di inmortales, obsecro uostram fidem, | ubi ego perii ? ubi inmutatus sum ? ubi ego formam perdidi ? | an egomet me illic reliqui, si forte oblitus fui ?*'

613. *walke*, beat. Cf. ll. 870, 972. Heywood, *A Mery Play* (ed. Whittingham, p. 3), 'Walke her cote.' *Ib.* p. 33, 'I have walkyd them well.' Heywood, *The fyrst hundred of Epigrammes*, 86 (ed. Spenser Society, p. 117), 'Thou wilt foole (quoth one) by [be?] walkt with a waster.' Shirburn Ballads (ed. Clark, p. 358), 'let blowes be walkinge.'

615. *curryed.* Palsgrave, 'I CURRY or beate. *Je bas, battre.*' Udall, *Floures for Latine Spekynge*, '*Verberibus casum te, &c.* I woll all to currie the, &c.' *Roister Doister*, I. iii. 77, 'a curried cote.' Skelton, *Magnyfycence*, 1641, 'coryed, beten, and blyst.'

622. *There was neuer Ape, &c.* Amph. 458, '*nam hicquidem omnem imaginem meam, quae antehac fuerat, possidet.*'

626. *Wyl he know me, &c.* Amph. 461, '*nisi etiam is quoque me ignorabit.*'

629. *cockes precius passion.* Cf. *The Four Elements* (Hazl. Dodsl. I. 25), 'Gog's passion.' Lindsay, *Three Estates*, 'Cokis passioun' (*passim*); *Hickscorner* (Hazl. Dodsl. I. 155, 156), 'Cock's passion.'

637. *dubtles.* Cf. *Roister Doister*, I. ii. 106, 'I am sorie God made me so comely doubtlesse.'

640. *let me alone.* Cf. *Roister Doister*, I. ii. 175, 'Yea now hardly lette me alone.'

648. *mome.* Cf. *Roister Doister*, III. ii. 86, &c. *Florio*, p. 81, 'A gull, a ninny, a mome, a sot.' *Comedy of Errors*, III. i. 32, 'Mome, malt-horse, capon, coxcomb, idiot, patch !'

653. *kyrie,*='kyrie eleison' (κύριε ἐλέησον). Cf. Heywood, *Proverbs* (Spenser Society, p. 64), 'She beginneth first with a cry a leysone' [i.e. a kyrie

eleison]. Bale, *Kynge Johan* (Camden Society, p. 98), 'He hath pipys and belles, with kyrye, kyrye, kyrye.' *A Supplycacion, &c.* (E.E.T.S. p. 69). Skelton, *Phyllyp Sparowe*, 379 ; *Colyn Cloute*, 755.   Nashe, *Have with you* (ed. McKerrow, p. 132), 'like a Crier, that when he hath done kire-elosoning it, puts of his cap, and cries God saue the Queene.' *Ib. Prayse of the Red Herring*, p. 209. Hazlitt unnecessarily emends to 'curry,' and Grosart explains as '=kyrre, quarry,—a hunting term = to cut up the deer.'

657. *corrasiue.* Cf. Udall, *Apophthegmes*, f. 154 b, 'What laude or thanke is he woorthie, saied *Diogenes*, that hauyng been so many yeres a studente contynually occupied in philosophie, hath yet hitherto geuen no bodye a corrosif ?'

658. *maisterishps*, i.e. maisterisshps, = 'mistress-ships.'

659. *sentence.* Cf. Barclay, *Ship of Fools* (ed. Jamieson, I. 137), 'his wordes, theyr sentence or intent.'

672. *graft.* Cf. *Nice Wanton* (Hazl. Dodsl. II. 173), 'Two graffs of an ill tree.' Gascoigne, *Supposes* (ed. Hazlitt, I. 206), 'grafts of such a stock.' Cf. 'imp.'

674. *breched*, literally 'put into breeches,' a metaphor for being put into the stocks. Cf. *Lear*, II. iv. 10, 'when a man's over-lusty at legs, then he wears wooden nether-stocks.' *Nether-stocks*=stockings, as *upper-stocks*=breeches. Cf. Heywood, *Epigrammes* (Spenser Society, p. 204), 'Thy vpper stocks be they stufte with sylke or flocks, Neuer become the lyke a nether payre of stocks' [i.e. being put in the stocks].

brake, i.e. the stocks. Cf. Udall, *Erasm. Par. Luke*, Pref. 6 b, 'So should I in this matier stand in a streight brake.' Shirley, *The Opportunity*, II. i., 'He is fallen into some brake, some wench has tied him by the legs.' (*N.E.D.*)

689. *vnhappye hooke.* Cf. ll. 116, 952. Skelton, *Magnyfycence*, 1390, 'For all hokes vnhappy to me haue resorte.' Heywood, *A Dialogue, &c.* (Spenser Society, p. 36), 'sens thou art crosse saylde, auale vnhappie hooke.'

700. *no force*, no matter. *Roister Doister*, IV. iii. 94 ; IV. vi. 44.

708. *I wine.* Cf. *Roister Doister*, I. iii. 100, 'chwine' = I ween.
I make god a vou. *Prompt. Parv.* 'A-VOWE. *Votum.*' 'A-WOWYN, or to make a-wowe. *Voveo.*'

711. *beat me.* No need to change to 'beaten,' with Hazlitt..

712. *tousing.* Cotgrave, 'Heruper. *To dischevel, towse, or disorder the hair ; to make it stare, or stand ill-favouredly.*' 'Housepillement : m. *A violent pulling, dragging, lugging, tugging, towsing.*'

725. *poumile.* Palsgrave, 'I POMELL, I beate one aboute the eares. *Je torche.*'

ioylile. 'Ioyly' is a favourite word with Udall. It occurs twice in *Roister Doister*, and 16 times in the *Apophthegmes*.

726. *wagepastie*, scapegrace. Cf. *Roister Doister*, III. ii. 10, 'a little wagpastie.' Heywood, *The Wise-woman of Hogsdon*, v. iv. (ed. Pearson, vol. v. p. 350), 'the wild vagaryes of this wanton wag pasty, a wild-oates I warrant him.' Cf. 'waghalter,' 'wagstring,' 'crackhalter,' 'crackrope.'

731. *lyeth gretylie me a pon.* Udall, *Floures for Latine Spekynge*, 'Scin ad te attinere hanc omnem rem?* Doest thou remembre that all this matter perteyneth to the? or lyeth the vppon?' *Roister Doister*, I. iv. 9, 'For this lieth vpon his preferment in deede.'

733. *dulines*, misprint for 'dullnes.' *Cath. Angl.* 'a DULLNES; *ebitudo*, *decliuitas.*'

735. *a paied*, satisfied, pleased. Cf. Golding, *Ovid's Met.* IV. 86, 'The sunne full ill appaid.' (*N.E.D.*)

736. *whan*, the M.E. form.

751. *canuased and tost.* Cotgrave, 'Berner. *To vanne or winnow corn; also, to canvass, or toss in a Sive; (a punishment inflicted on such as commit gross absurdities).*

759. *marchent*, rogue. Udall, *Apophthegmes*, f. 252, 'lustie young ruffleers and wylde merchauntes.' Heywood, *Proverbs* (Spenser Society, p. 26), 'Ye marchant, what attempth you, &c.' For the character of merchants, v. Lindesay, *Ane Satyre* (E.E.T.S.), *vv.* 4034—4087; *The Three Ladies of London* (Hazl. Dodsl. VI. 275—8); *Piers the Plowman*, B-text, VII. 18—22. The word occurs also in this sense in *The History of Jacob and Esau* (Hazl. Dodsl. II. 255); *New Custom* (ib. III. 8); *Marriage of Wit and Science* (ib. II. 383); *Conflict of Conscience* (ib. VI. 54).

763. *calphe.* Cf. *Roister Doister*, II. iv. 10, 'You great calfe'; III. iii. 17, 'Ye are such a calfe, such an asse, such a blocke.' v. Cotgrave s.v. *veau.*

777. The 'I' at the end of the line is inverted.

781. *payne.* Hazlitt unnecessarily inserts a semicolon.

784. *Why ye naughtye villaine, &c.* Amph. 566, 'tune id dicere audes, quod nemo umquam homo antehac | uidit nec potest fieri, tempore uno | homo idem duobus locis ut simul sit?'

788. *drankest thou, &c.* Amph. 576, 'ubi bibisti?'

789. *I shreue me.* Palsgrave, 'I SHREWE one, I beshrewe him. *Je mauldis.*'

791. *dranke.* Palsgrave, 'I drinke, I suffer correctyon for a faulte. *Je compaire.*' *Roister Doister*, I. iii. 29, 'drink without a cup.' *The History of Jacob and Esau* (Hazl. Dodsl. II. 254), 'ye shall drink of the whip.' Lyly, *Mydas*, I. ii. *ad fin.*, 'drinke of a drie cuppe.' *Thersites* (Hazl. Dodsl. I. 411), 'I will make thee drink worse than good ale.' Gascoigne, *Steel Glas* (ed.

Arber, p. 68), 'drinke vpon the whippe.' Cf. Heywood, *Epigrammes* (ed. Spenser Society, p. 215).

798. *What you saucye, &c.* Amph. 565, '*tun me, uerbero, audes erum ludificari ?*'

800. *your tonge is lyberall, &c.* Amph. 556, '*iam quidem hercle ego tibi istam | scelestam, scelus, linguam abscidam.*'

lyberall. Cf. *Hamlet,* IV. vii. 171.

801. *counger.* Cf. l. 108.

803. *chrystendome,* baptism. *Cath. Angl.* 'a CRYSTENDAM ; *baptismus, baptisma, christianitas, christianismus.*' Wyclif, *Works,* iii. 285, speaks of the sacrament of '*cristendom*' (Herrtage). *Piers Plowman,* B-text, XI. 120, 'For though a Crystene man coueyted his Crystendome to reneye.'

807. *toyes.* Read 'thy toyes.'

pranke. Read 'prankes.'

808. *And now thou art, &c.* Amph. 585, '*sequere sis, erum qui ludificas dictis delirantibus : | qui quoniam erus quod imperauit neglexisti persequi, | nunc uenis etiam ultro inrisum dominum : quae neque fieri | possunt neque fando umquam accepit quisquam, profers, carnufex : | quoius ego hodie in tergum faxo ista expetant mendacia.*'

818. *Loo is not he, &c.* Amph. 590, '*Amphitruo, miserruma istaec miseriast seruo bono, | apud erum qui uera loquitur, si id ui uerum uincitur.*'

825. *Nay I maruael, &c.* Amph. 596, '*nilo, inquam, mirum magis tibi istuc quam mihi : | neque, ita me di ament, credebam primo mihimet Sosiae, | donec Sosia me ille egomet fecit sibi uti crederem.*'

826. *meaue. Prompt. Parv.* 'MEVYN̄, or steryn̄. *Moveo.*' Palsgrave, 'I MEVE or styrre by anger. *Je esmeus.*'

833. *That thou laiest doune, &c.* Amph. 620, '*num obdormiuisti dudum?... ibi forte istum si uidisses quendam in somnis Sosiam.*'

sleppest. The verb 'to sleep' was originally strong, and the past tense 'slep' is still used in dialects.

840. *as fast as a bere in a cage.* Cf. *Digby Mysteries* (ed. Furnivall, p. 10), 'as fers as a lyon in a cage.' Heywood, *Proverbs* (Spenser Society, p. 43), 'As comely as is a cowe in a cage.' Nashe, *Have with You* (ed. McKerrow, III. 43). In the *Ancren Riwle,* p. 198, the bear is the type of sloth.

840—1. Amph. 622, '*non soleo ego somniculose eri imperia persequi.*'

843. *I sawe and felte it as waking, &c.* Amph. 623, '*uigilans uidi, uigilans nunc uideo, uigilans fabulor, | uigilantem ille me iam dudum uigilans pugnis contudit.*'

844. *soner,* the M.E. form.

850. *Why then thou speakest not, &c.* Amph. 616, '*sed uidistin uxorem meam ?*'

851. *No that I dyd not, &c.* Amph. 617, '*quin intro ire in aedis numquam licitumst.*'

855. *the dyuell neuer so beate his dame.* Cf. *Grim the Collier of Croyden; or, The Devil and his Dame* (Hazl. Dodsl. VIII. 400), 'Now is Belphegor, an incarnate devil, Come to the earth to seek him out a dame.' *Ib.* 452, 'He [i.e. Belphegor] thinks to overcrow me [i.e. his dame] with words and blows.'

856. *And where became, &c.* Amph. 619, '*quis istic Sosiast ?*'

where became. Udall, *Apophthegmes,* f. 66, 'where is now that your greate high frendship become ?' *Hickscorner* (Hazl. Dodsl. I. 176), 'Where be the traitors become now ?' *The Three Ladies of London* (Hazl. Dodsl. VI. 360), 'thou knowest where they are become.'

859. *for .xl. pens.* *A C. Mery Talys, lxvi.* (ed. Hazlitt, p. 94), 'John Dawe......layde with his curate for a wager xl. pence.' *The Turnament of Totenham* (Hazlitt's Early Popular Poetry, III. 90), 'An hors for xl. penys.'

861. *rape thee.* *Roister Doister,* III. v. 93, 'Yea and rappe you againe.'

870. *walke his cote.* Cf. ll. 613, 972.

871. *ladi.* Cf. 'ladye,' l. 385.

873. *I had rather thē .xl. pens.* Cf. *Trial of Treasure* (Hazl. Dodsl. III. 281), 'I had rather than forty pence that he were come.'

878. *a other.* Read 'ā other.'

879. *heauen quene.* Cf. Chaucer, *An A.B.C.,* 24, 'blisful hevene quene.' *Ib.* 149, 'O hevene queen.' O.E. *heofena.*

884. A line has been lost before this.

886. *as iust as .iiii. pens to a grot.* Amph. 601, '*neque lac lactis magis est simile quam ille ego similest mei.*' Ray, *English Proverbs* (ed. 1768, p. 224), 'As like as fourpence to a groat.'

891. *looke him.* Cf. Lindesay, *Ane Satyre* (E.E.T.S.), 3417, 'gif zow list cum and luik it.' *Beues of Hamtoun* (E.E.T.S.), 1439, 'ffor all the tresoure, That I myght in this toure loke.'

894. *he called hym selfe by my owne name.* Amph. 600, '*formam una abstulit cum nomine.*'

895. *tolde me all that I haue done.* Amph. 599, '*ordine omne, uti quicque actumst, dum apud hostis sedimus, | edissertauit.*'

898. *you send me home, &c.* Amph. 602, '*nam ut dudum ante lucem a portu me praemisisti domum.*'

900. *Bukelers.* Cf. l. 135.

904. *Thou shalt haue by therfore.* Read 'abye.' Cf. l. 206, 'thou wolt shurlie abye.' *Roister Doister,* II. iv. 21, 'full truly abye thou shalt.' Or, read 'why' for 'by.' Cf. *Johan the Euangelyst* (ed. Malone Society), 61, 'Ye shulde haue well why.'

W. J. J.   5

907. *Laye on, &c.* Cf. the Host's wife in Chaucer, *C. T.*, B, 3083—3090, 'By goddes bones ! whan I bete my knaves, She bringth me forth the grete clobbed staves, And cryeth, "slee the dogges everichoon, And brek hem, bothe bak and every boon."'

908. *Joll.* Palsgrave, 'I JOLLE one aboute the eares. *Je soufflette*, prim. conj. I jolled hym aboute the eares tyll I made my fyste sore' [which explains 'fauoure your fyste'].

fauoure. Udall, *Floures*, '*tibi parce*, fauour or spare your selfe.'

913. *I haue had betyng, &c.* Amph. 606, '*nam sum obtusus pugnis pessume.*'

914. *Careawayne*, influenced by the terminations of ll. 911—12, 915—16.

918. *I me beat me thus.* Amph. 607, '*egomet memet*' [*sc. uerberaui*].

919. *he I.* Amph. 625, '*Sosia, inquam, ego ille.*'

923. *churles knaue.* Cf. Chaucer, *C. T.*, A, 3169, 'cherles tale.' *Ib.* D, 2206, 'cherles dede.'

925. *verye wel.* Hazlitt omits 'wel.'

933. *pigesnie.* *Roister Doister*, I. iv. 42 ; III. iv. 32. Chaucer, *C. T.*, A, 3268, 'She was a prymerole, a pigges-nye' (with Skeat's note). *The Rare Triumphs of Love and Fortune* (Hazl. Dodsl. VI. 222). *Locrine*, I. ii. (ed. Tauchnitz, p. 141). Cf. 'O my sweet birds-nie,' *The City Nightcap* (Hazl. Dodsl. XIII. 124 ; *ib.* 141, 142). Cf. Plautus, *Poen.* 366 '*meus ocellus.*'

934. *hange vppe.* Cf. *Gammer Gurton's Needle*, III. iii. 11, 'Give thee thy right and hang thee up.' *The Pardoner and the Friar* (E.E.D.S. p. 15), 'I had liever thou were hanged up with a rope.'

952. *vnhappye hooke.* Cf. l. 689.

959. *vere*, spring. Skelton, *On Tyme*, 24 (ed. Dyce, I. p. 138), 'The rotys take theyr sap in tyme of vere.'

963. *Peres.* The M.E. spelling.

968. *waister*, cudgel. See Nares, *s.v.* 'Waster.' Hazlitt and Grosart print 'master' without comment.

969. *ere.* Hazlitt changes to 'here.'

972. *walke his cote.* Cf. ll. 613, 870.

974. *Calycow.* Cf. Sidney, *Apologie for Poetrie* (ed. Shuckburgh, p. 53), 'I may speake (though I am heere) of Peru, and in speech digresse from that to the description of Calicut.' Bailey, 'CALICOE, a sort of Cloth made of Cotton brought from *Calicut*, a Town of the Kingdom of *Malibar*, in the *East Indies*.'

975. *bedelem.* Cf. l. 498.

976. *hence to Iherusalem.* Cf. *Roister Doister*, IV. vii. 60, 'the best hennes to grece.' Heywood, *A Mery Play* (ed. Whittingham, p. 9), 'the

most bawde hens to Coventrie.' *Proverbs* (Spenser Society, p. 25), 'Not a more gagglyng gander hense to Chester.'

981. *shit vp.* Cf. Udall, *Floures,* 'Shit faste the doore with bothe the boltes.'

985. *maister.* Read 'maisters.'

I best. Read 'it best.' The misprint i due to the 'I' immediately above.

992. *lesse,* lose. Read 'leese.'

994. *the Catte winked when here iye was out.* Cf. Heywood, *Proverbs* (Spenser Society, p. 50), 'But somwhat it is, I see, when the cat wynkth, And bothe hir eyne out, but further stryfe to shonne, Let the cat winke, and leat the mouse ronne.' *The World and the Child* (Hazl. Dodsl. I. 265), 'Ah, ah, sirs, let the cat wink.' *Appius and Virginia* (Hazl. Dodsl. IV. 152), 'Nay, stay, I pray you, and let the cat wink.' Skelton, *Colyn Cloute,* 459, 'With, Let the cat wynke.'

996. *sum Englyshe maye be piked therof out,* i.e. some modern application may be discovered. Cf. Nashe, *Prayse of the Red Herring* (ed. McKerrow, III. 195), 'Many of you haue read these stories, and coulde neuer picke out any such English.'

1005. *moune is made of a grene chese.* Cf. Hazlitt, *English Proverbs,* ed. 1882, p. 392.

1011. *pfit.* The stroke through the tail of the *p* is an abbreviation of *-er.* Sometimes the symbol stands for *par.*

1013. *good maister.* Cf. *Roister Doister,* IV. vii. 100, 'Be good maister to her.' Skelton, *Magnyfycence,* 808, 'Why dost thou not supplye, And desyre me thy good maynster to be?' Shakespeare, *The Winter's Tale,* V. ii. *ad fin.*

1017. *han,* is found in Chaucer and Langland as a present plural but not singular.

1019. *the Croue is whight.* Cf. Heywood, *Proverbs* (Spenser Society, p. 56), 'Were not you as good than to say, the crow is whight.' Gifford, *A Posie of Gilloflowers* (Miscellanies of the Fuller Worthies' Library, I. 369) 'I cannot say the crow is white, But needes must call a spade a spade.' Andrew, *Anatomie of Basenesse* (ib. II. 27), 'Haue I not heard one tell the crowe shee's white?' Juvenal, III. 30, '*maneant qui nigrum in candida uertunt.*' Ovid, *Met.* XI. 314. λευκὸς κόραξ was proverbial.

1024. *arrierage.* Cf. Langland, *Piers the Plowman,* C-text, X. 274, '*Redde rationem uillicacionis tue*·other in arerage falle.' Chaucer, *C. T.,* A, 602, 'Ther coude no man bringe him in arrerage.'

1028. *put in vre.* Palsgrave, 'I put in ure. *Je mets en experience,* or *je mets en trayn.*'

1031. *gaine.* Read 'game.'

1039. *togithers.* So 'togideres' in *Piers the Plowman*, B-text, I. 195, II. 83.

1053. *Baryng him selfe in hand.* Palsgrave, 'I beare in hande, I threp upon a man that hath done a dede or make him byleve so.' 'I beare hym in hande he was wode.' *Je luy metz sus la raige*, or *je luy metz sus quil estoyt enragé.*'

1060. *gidaū.* The final *-ce* is omitted.

1068. *newe yere.* See note on l. 84.

APPENDIX

FRAGMENT OF A LATER EDITION

(ll. 696—802.)

For he tolde me when he foorth went :
That thou shouldst come back again incontinent.
To bring me to supper where he now is :
And thou hast played by the way and they haue doon by this
But no force I shall thou maist trust me :
Teache all naughtie knaues to beware by thee.

❧ Careaway.

Forsooth mistres if you knew as muche as I :
You would not be with me halfe so angry.
For the fault is neyther in my maister, nor in me, nor you
But in another knaue that was heer euen now.
And his name was Jenkin Careaway.

❧ Dame Coy.

What ? I see my man is disposed to play.
I ween he be druncken or mad I make God a vow :

❧ Careaway.

Nay I haue been made sober and tame I now.
I was neuer so handled before in all my life :
I would euery man in England had so beaten his wife.
I haue forgotten with tousing by the hear :
What I deuised to say a little ere.

❧ Dame Coy.

Haue I lost my supper this night through thy negligēce :

❧ Careaway.

Nay then were I a knaue sauing your reuerence.

❧ Dame Coy.

Why ? I am sure that by this time it is doon :

5—3

❡ Careaway.

Yea that it was more then an houre agone.

❡ Dame Coy.

And wast not thou sent to fetche me thither :

❡ Careaway.

Yes and had come right quickly hither.
But that by the way I had a great fall :
And my name, body, shape, legges and all.
And met with one that from me did it steal :
By by God first he and I some blowes did deal.
I would he were present now before your gate :
For you could pummel him ioylyly about the pate.

❡ Dame Coy.

Truly this wagpastie is eyther drunck or mad :

❡ Careaway.

Neuer man suffred so muche wrong as I had.
But mistres I should say a thing to you :
Tary it wil come to my remembrance euen now.
I must needs vse a substantiall premeditation :
For the matter lyeth greatly me vpon.
I beseeche your mistreship of pardon and forgiuenes :
Desyring you to impute it to my simple and rude dulnes.
I haue forgotten what I haue thought to haue said :
And am therof ful il apaid.
But when I lost my self this mischaunce also fel :
I lost also that I should you tel.

❡ Dame Coy.

Why thou wretched villain doost thou me scorn and mock :
To make me to these folke a laughing stock.
Ere thou go out of my hands thou shalt haue some thing
    I wil recken better in the morning.

❡ Careaway.

    beat me maistres aduise you :
    none of your seruants now.
    er I is now your page :
        longer in your bondage.

¶ Dame Coy.

Now walke precious theef get thee out of my sight :
And come no more in my presence this night.
Get thee hence and wait on thy maister at once :

¶ Careaway.

Mary sir this is handling for the nonce.
I would I had been hanged before that I was lost :
I was neuer this canuased and tost.
That if my maister on his part also :
Handle me as my mistres and the other I doo.
I shall surely be killed between them three :
And all the deuils in hel shall not saue me.
But yet if the other I might with me haue part :
All this would neuer greeue my hart.

¶ Jugler.

How say you maisters I pray you tel :
Haue not I requited my marchant wel ?
Haue not I handled him after a good sorte :
Had it not been pittie to haue lost this sporte.
Anon his maister on his behalfe :
You shall see how he wil handle the Calfe.
For if he throughly an angred be :
He wil make him smart so mote I thee.
I would not for the price of a new pair of shoon :
That any parte of this had been vndoon.
Wel, sith that now reuenged is my quarel :
I wil go doo of mine apparel.
And now let Careaway be Careaway again :
I haue doon with that name now certain.
Except peraduenture I shall take the self same weed :
Some other time again for a like cause and need.

¶ Boungrace.

Why then dare thou to presume to tel me :
That I knowe is no wise possible for to be ?

¶ Careaway.

Now by my truthe maister I haue tolde no lie.
And all these folke knowe as wel as I.

I had no sooner knocked at the gate :
But straight wayes he had me by the pate.
Therfore if you beat me til I fart and shite again :
You shall not cause me for any pain.
But I wil affirm as I said before :
That when I came neer another stood at the door.

❡ Maister Boungrace.

Why thou naughtie villain darest thou affirm to me ?
That whiche was neuer seen nor heer after shalbe ?
That one man may haue two bodies and two faces ?
And that one man at one time may be in two places ?
Tel me, drankest thou any where by the way ?

❡ Careaway.

Beshrew me if I dranck any more then twise to day :
Til I met euen now with that other I :
And with him I supped and drank truly.
But as for you if you gaue me drinck and meat :
As oftentimes as you doo me beat.
I were the best fed page in all this Cittie.
But as touching that you haue on me no pittie.
And not onely   that doo you serue :
For meat and drinck may rather starue.

❡ Maister Boungrace.

What you saucy malapart knaue :
Begin you with your maister to prate and raue ?
Your tung is liberall and all out of frame :
I must needs coniure it and make it tame
Wher is that other Careaway that thou saydst was heer

NOTE.   Where *lacunae* occur the original is torn or rubbed.

INDEX TO THE NOTES

good maister 1013
George, saint 317
graft 672
grudgid 262

halpeny worth of siluer spoons 218
hange vppe 934
hardelye 362
haue by therfore 904
he-I 919
heauen quene 879
heele, out at 349
hei hei 200
hooke 689

I-thou 524, 550
ieopard 318
ioll 908
ioylile 725
iugling cast 107

Jenkine 114
Jhone, sainte 84

kyrie 653

ladye boons, our 385
laye on 907
life, giue my 249
looke him 891
lookes 341
lyberall 800
lyeth apon 731
lyne 211

marchent 759
marcy, crye you 471
meaue 826
merie and glad 69
minceth 228
mome 648
moull 108
moune made of grene chese 1005
muse 308
my simithe 191
my thought 258

nere 410

niddes 17
no poynt 482
nod 479
nomine patris 430
nons, for the 177
notted 575
nowne 422

offirme 46
or 81
our ladye boons 385
Ouyd 28
oyster shel 61

parat Poppagaye 235
pecpours 592
percace 7
pigesnie 933
pike 421
Plautus 64
potstike 148
poumile 725
prankith 226
precious 148, 590

quesie 66

rage 441
rape 861
rest you merye 85
romeringe 461
rufflers 269

scentence 65
sentence 659
set by 267, 345
shit vp 981
shreue, I 789
simperith 226
sleppest 833
slinking 590
snache, God me 414
soft 331
souse 423
spoons, halpeny worth of siluer 218
starke staryng 181
Steuen, saint 86
stinke, beate tyll I 496

straus, cople of 395
stoding 310
swere and stare 163
swete mete 323
swimmeth 228
syr 293

thee, so mote I 492
togithers 1039
tousing 712
tredith 229
truce for a whyle 486
tryppeth 229

vengable 219
verament 32

vnhappy 116, 689
vre, put in 1028

wage 116
wagepastie 726
waghith 384
walke 421, 613, 870
wardelith 231
where became 856
whether 183
wine, I 708
wine shakin 592
witts fiue 584
wood 369
wrong, had 147

CAMBRIDGE: PRINTED BY JOHN CLAY, M.A. AT THE UNIVERSITY PRESS